Counseling With Youth

OTHER BOOKS BY DR. NARRAMORE . . .

The "Christian Psychology" Series

How to Tell Your Children About Sex

How to Understand and Influence Children

Life and Love

The Psychology of Counseling

This Way to Happiness

A Woman's World

Young Only Once

Encyclopedia of Psychological Problems

Counseling
With
Youth

at Church, School and Camp

by Clyde M. Narramore, Ed. D.

ZONDERVAN PUBLISHING COMPANY
GRAND RAPIDS, MICHIGAN

CONTENTS

Counseling With Youth

1

The Importance and Urgency of Counseling

As YOU TURN the pages of Scripture you find that God usually uses people to help people.

The raising of Lazarus is an excellent example of the principle behind Christian counseling.

> Now Jesus again sighing repeatedly *and* deeply disquieted, approached the tomb. It was a cave — a hole in the rock — and a boulder lay against [the entrance to close] it.
>
> Jesus said, Take away the stone. Martha, the sister of the dead man, exclaimed, But Lord, by this time he [is decaying and] throws off an offensive odor, for he has been dead four days!
>
> Jesus said to her, Did I not tell you *and* promise you that if you would believe *and* rely on Me, you should see the glory of God?
>
> So they took away the stone. And Jesus lifted up His eyes and said, Father, I thank You that You have heard Me.
>
> Yes, I know You always hear and listen to Me; but I have said this on account of *and* for the benefit of the people standing around, so that they may believe You did send Me — that You have made Me Your Messenger.
>
> When He had said this, He shouted with a loud voice, Lazarus, come out!
>
> And out walked the man who had been dead, his hands and feet wrapped in burial cloths (linen strips), and with a [burial] napkin bound around his face.

Jesus said to them, Free him of the burial wrappings and let him go (John 11:38-44, *Amplified Bible*).

Now that Lazarus was raised from the dead Christ could have done several things. He could have said, "Lazarus, what is the matter? I have raised you from death but you just stand there bound in graveclothes." But Christ didn't choose to condemn Lazarus, nor does He condemn the new Christian for old habits and emotional problems from the unconverted life.

A second alternative is that Christ could have removed the graveclothes. He had shown the power to overcome death, surely He could remove these graveclothes. But Christ did not choose to perform this miracle. Neither does Christ miraculously take away all our emotional and physical problems at the time of salvation.

Instead of either of these two alternatives Christ turned and said, "Free him of the burial wrappings and let him go." Christ didn't condemn Lazarus. He did not miraculously remove the graveclothes. *He used other individuals to do this.*

This is a good example of what God does in counseling. He does the forgiving and healing, but He uses counselors to take off the binding graveclothes so that people can be freed from the shackle of damaged emotions. What a privilege to be used of God to free people!

THE IMPORTANCE OF COUNSELING

Your counseling is significant because *people need help which they can't get from a group!* They need an individual approach. Counseling focuses on individual needs.

It also allows for *two-way communication.* When you talk to a group you do most of the speaking: the audience listens. But in personal counseling the counselor does most of the listening, and the counselee is encouraged to talk. In this way the counselee can express himself, get rid of strong feelings, clarify his thinking and consider various solutions.

As a Christian counselor *you are God's representative.* You can help and influence people immeasurably. The things you do and say, coupled with your attitudes, can profoundly affect those with whom you counsel.

Take Bill, for example. It was during those first days at camp that he came face to face with the realization that Jesus Christ died for him — personally.

As a counselor spoke to him one night Bill said, "I have never accepted Jesus Christ but I feel that I should. I really want to. Right now."

The counselor, though young, was wise. He pointed out certain Scripture passages, and encouraged Bill to take the step. At that moment Bill opened his heart and asked the Lord to come in and take charge of his life.

When Bill came back from camp he was a different person. He began to make new plans for the future. II Corinthians 5:17 had become a reality to him:

> Therefore if any person is (ingrafted) in Christ, the Messiah, he is (a new creature altogether,) a new creation; the old (previous moral and spiritual condition) has passed away. Behold, the fresh *and* new has come! (*Amplified Bible*).

The counseling Bill received at camp truly did affect his entire life.

Elaine is another illustration. Although she was a believer, she had a serious problem with her mother. "I simply can't stand my mother," she told her counselor. "We fight all the time. What's the use of going to church, acting like everything's o.k., then coming home and yelling at each other all week?"

The counselor wisely led Elaine into discussions about the hostility she held toward her mother. In fact, they talked it over several times. And before long Elaine developed a new insight into the problem. With this new insight came a change of attitude toward her parents. The counselor helped Elaine to utilize resources available in Christ. Little wonder, then, that Elaine's home life soon changed radically.

Many counselors have been used mightily of God to bring help to young people such as Bill and Elaine.

THE URGENCY OF COUNSELING

There is a real urgency in counseling since *the youth you deal with will be young only once.* Later they will not be easy to influence. Next year they will be a little older, perhaps more worldly-wise and less receptive than they are now.

Consider this, too: *If you don't give young people the help they need now, they may never get it from any other source!* Some have been raised in homes where there is disharmony and disunity; homes where the Bible is not honored and applied to daily living. And unless you, a Christian counselor, help them with their needs and answer their questions, they may *never* find real solutions.

There is also great urgency in your counseling, since without help *their difficulties will become worse.* Problems don't just solve themselves. They usually become more exaggerated and more serious. Later they will require a longer period of time to solve.

If your counseling has the setting of a camp, so much the better. Such an atmosphere is usually ideal. Besides the out-of-doors setting, there is good food and plenty of activity: hiking, swimming, boating and all that goes with it.

In addition, there are times of singing and witnessing when God can deal with young people in a special way. Also, at camp the young people are removed from their families. They are away from the gang. And, for once, they are in a place where they can — and probably will — really consider their problems.

Up to this time some of these young people may not have even realized the true seriousness of their problems. Some of them have been on the go constantly. Many of them have carried transistor radios to help divert their minds. At school they are occupied with activities. At home they have television or study. At church (if they attend) they may look at photographs, pass notes or whisper instead of listening to the minister. Now for the first time these young people have time to think. And they do think. There is something about the mountains, the smell of the pine trees and oaks, the pounding of the surf, that dispells the thin veneer of sophistication in which most young people try to hide themselves.

Young people often confide in a counselor when they will not seek help from their own parents or pastors. Relationships with Mom and Dad may be strained, but not with a young counselor. This is partially due to the camp atmosphere and partially because their relationship with you has not been spoiled by any previous experience or image. Though they may appear guarded at first, they really are quite open to you and your counseling. So counsel with confidence.

Young Counselors

Sometimes a counselor who is quite young feels that he may not do a good job because of his age. As one inexperienced counselor put it, "Sometimes I feel so foolish counseling with kids who are almost my age."

If you feel this way, just remember that people may find you easier to talk to than those who are older. One time I was talking to a young lady who had been selected Miss America. She had traveled across the United States many times and had met many people. As we sat chatting, I asked her what most people talked to her about.

"Problems," she replied unhesitatingly. "No matter where I go or what I am doing — riding on a plane, sitting with 'big shots' at banquets, or attending fancy functions, men and women in their forties, fifties and sixties start talking to me about their problems. Think of it — they ask me — a twenty-year-old — what they should do about their problems!"

Undoubtedly the reason they talked to her about problems was because they were burdened and *she* would listen.

So it is with you. You may not have many gray hairs — in fact you may still be a teen-ager, but if you will listen, people will bring their problems to you. And if you have godly wisdom, you can help them.

Remember the Apostle Paul's advice to young Timothy:

Let no one despise *or* think less of you because of your youth, but be an example (pattern) for the believers, in speech, in conduct, in love, in faith and in purity (I Timothy 4:12, *Amplified Bible*).

No matter what your age is, you have an appeal right now which you will not have later. You can also reach a certain age group which you may never be able to reach again.

Remember that some of the men and women whom God has

used the most were young when God used them. Consider
David. He was only a young man when he slew the giant.
Think of Joseph. He too was young when thrown into the pit by
his brothers, then sold as a slave to the Egyptians. But remem-
ber how wondrously God used him. Then there was Daniel.
And so on. . .

Some of the great art masterpieces of all times were painted
by young men still in their teens. One time I was traveling in
Rome, Italy. One of the first sights I saw was the world-famous
Borghese Museum, high on a hill overlooking the eternal city.
There I viewed some of the finest oil paintings and sculpture
known to man. Our guide patiently explained each work of art,
discussing in some detail the great master who had created it.
You can imagine my amazement when upon asking the curator
the age of the "master" when he did his great work, he often
replied, "eighteen" or "nineteen."

Some of today's greatest athletes or Olympic champions are
not yet twenty. So consider your own youthfulness as an asset
rather than a liability.

Keep this in mind: You will not be counseling alone — God
is with you. Consider these words written by James the Apostle,
and brother of our Lord, "If any of you lack wisdom, let him ask
of God, that giveth to all men liberally, and upbraideth not; and
it shall be given him" (James 1:5).

Meditate upon the promise given in Hebrews 4:16, "Let us
therefore come boldly unto the throne of grace, that we may
obtain mercy, and find grace to help in time of need." So
counsel with confidence and claim this promise: "For I will give
you a mouth and wisdom, which all your adversaries shall not
be able to gainsay nor resist" (Luke 21:15).

Your counseling is important. You are working with human
souls who will be somewhere forever. And *your counseling is
urgent.* Realize, when you help a person, that you may never
have the opportunity again.

QUESTIONS FOR DISCUSSION

1. What is accomplished through individual counseling that may not be achieved through speaking to a group?

2. What is the significance of the Biblical account of the raising of Lazarus as it applies to counseling?

3. What is meant by two-way communication in counseling?

4. How can a counselor be God's representative?

5. Discuss the urgency of counseling.

6. Discuss the possibility of serious problems resolving themselves.

7. Why might a young person respond to a counselor who is not a member of his family, when he would not respond to his own parents?

8. What does the setting of a camp have to do with the response a young person may have to counseling?

9. How might a young, somewhat inexperienced counselor feel about counseling others?

10. Give several examples of young people who have been used of God in significant ways.

11. How do you feel about counseling those who are older than you?

12. In what ways do you need to improve in order to become a better counselor?

2

What Counseling Will Do for You

It is interesting, but true, that those who help others, help themselves.

I have noticed this each year at the international headquarters of the Narramore Christian Foundation where we offer one year internships to men who have completed advanced degrees in psychology. Invariably, these top young men grow and develop as they counsel with others. I'll never forget what one intern told me after three months of training.

"What general insights are you gaining about your clients?" I asked.

"I'm not sure just what I'm learning about other people," he replied, "but I am learning a lot about myself. Each evening as I drive home from the office I keep thinking of my clients in relation to my own development. When I counsel with a person I am usually reminded of something in my own life which needs to be improved upon."

And so it is. As we are brought face to face with the dynamics in the lives of others we usually begin to understand why we, ourselves, act as we do. Jim, for example, had never thought much about the causes of his own behavior. But after he had counseled one summer at camp, he began to get a clearer picture of why he acted and reacted as he did. This insight naturally led to better understanding — and change.

Counseling will help you to become more outgoing — more interested in others — a better conversationalist. Since counseling is comprised basically of expressing one's feelings verbally, you will naturally become skilled in conversation. You will learn why people ask questions; why, on the other hand, they avoid certain topics. You will learn how to restrain yourself. You will come to understand, too, when you should enter into conversation and when to raise questions. All of these skills gained in counseling will enable you to be more effective both in public and in private.

Experience in counseling will naturally help you to become a more thoughtful parent and teacher. Through your counseling you will understand why marriage problems develop — and how to avoid them. As you help a counselee trace his attitudes back to childhood experiences, you will become a wiser parent yourself. You will be able to work more effectively with your own sons and daughters or other children whom you are teaching.

Counseling will also help you to become more spiritually mature. The Bible says, "For in him we live, and move, and have our being . . ." (Acts 17:28). In other words, God is central in the behavior of mankind. Primarily, we act as we do because of our relationship to Christ and God. Since counseling is concerned with God's creatures, their relationships to each other and to God, counselors should have the mind of God. This can be achieved through understanding and obeying God's Word — the Bible. As you draw upon the Word to help others, you will naturally grow yourself.

It is utterly beyond man's comprehension to understand the complete benefits of the Word of God as it relates to human problems. But it *is* the counselor's joy and privilege to use it! Consider briefly, the following dynamics as the Bible engages the heart of man:

The Word of God reaches into the depths of a man's being and *convicts* him — convicts him of that which separates him from God. "Come now, and let us reason together, saith the LORD: though your sins be as scarlet, they shall be as white as snow; though they be red like crimson, they shall be as wool" (Isaiah 1:18).

The Bible also brings *regeneration* through the message of salvation. In Titus 3:5 we read, "Not by works of righteousness which we have done, but according to his mercy he saved us, by the washing of regeneration, and renewing of the Holy Ghost." All that man can accomplish through secular psychology and psychiatry is as nothing when compared to spiritual conversion. Who but the Holy Spirit can change man's nature and give him new desires and appetites?

The Word of God produces *faith,* practical faith with which to live each day. The Bible enters into a heart of unbelief and fills it to overflowing with faith. "So then faith cometh by hearing, and hearing by the word of God" (Romans 10:17).

The Word also offers *cleansing* for the believer. "If we confess our sins, he is faithful and just to forgive us our sins, and to cleanse us from all unrighteousness" (I John 1:9). No longer does man need to walk with soiled feet and a guilty conscience.

The Word gives us unerring *guidance.* God, Himself, says, "I will instruct thee and teach thee in the way which thou shalt go: I will guide thee with mine eye" (Psalm 32:8). The sincere follower of Christ is not left to wander aimlessly or to follow the whims of a confused and vascillating twentieth-century society.

The Word of God offers *protection* against sin. Evil not only abounds; it destroys. It robs a person of his emotional and mental well-being. But Christ overcomes evil: "Thy word have I hid in mine heart, that I might not sin against thee" (Psalm 119:11).

The experienced Christian counselor knows, too, that God's Word brings *comfort* to each longing heart. When sorrows overwhelm and burdens seem too heavy to bear, the Comforter comes to bring peace and hope. "Who comforteth us in all our tribulations, that we may be able to comfort them which are in any trouble, by the comfort wherewith we ourselves are comforted of God" (II Corinthians 1:4).

All of these — and more — are wrought through the Word of God, and the counselor who knows and uses the Bible, grows immeasurably.

In summary, counseling can do much for you. Your sensitivity to other people, your understanding of problems, and your reliance on Christ will enrich your own life.

Questions for Discussion

1. Why might a counselor lack insight into his own problems until he sees the same dynamics at work in the life of his counselee?

2. How can counseling experiences help the counselor to become more outgoing with improved conversation skills?

3. Discuss the benefits to the counselor of using God's Word in counseling.

4. Discuss ways, other than those presented in this chapter, in which the counselor can develop from his experiences in counseling.

5. Which ideas presented in this chapter are the most significant to you?

3
The Successful Counselor

PEOPLE OFTEN ASK, "What is the most important thing in counseling?"

The answer is, "The counselor."

Your techniques and training are essential, but more important is your own personal adjustment. You may have wide experience and depth of knowledge, but without adequate personal qualities these are of little value. Let's look, then, at some of the most important qualities of a successful counselor.

An effective counselor is a well-adjusted individual. Although you cannot expect to be free from all personality weaknesses, it is important that you have no severe emotional conflicts. When a person is struggling with his own adjustment, he is not free to reach out to the needs and interests of others. Jim, for example, was a college student counseling at a summer camp. He loved the Lord and was interested in the campers, but had a serious problem with his temper. The slightest frustration would set Jim into a whirl of activity and hostility. He would ridicule the campers in his cabin and tell them how foolish and childish they were. Needless to say, no one came to Jim for counseling. They knew that he couldn't handle his own adjustment, much less another person's.

Understanding of one's own behavior is important in dealing with others. An effective counselor has considerable insight into his own feelings and actions. This self-understanding is important to you for two major reasons. First, it prevents you from trying to solve your own problems when counseling with others. The person who is unaware of his own weakness can easily project his problems on to the counselee rather than focusing on the counselee's real problem.

A second benefit of self-insight is the understanding this gives into the adjustment of others. Since everyone has basically the same emotional and spiritual needs, an understanding of one's self aids in understanding others. Care must be taken, however, not to attribute recklessly your conflicts to others nor to assume that a solution which has benefited you will always have like value for another. Every person is an individual and must be dealt with as such.

People show their emotional adjustment in many ways. The table on page 22 lists a number of characteristics of emotional and mental well-being. By placing a check mark in the appropriate rating you can gain a better view of your adjustment. You may also want to ask a close friend to rate you on these same traits.

How did you rate? If your scores were largely fours and fives, excellent! If you have a number of ratings of one and two you should seriously consider these weaker areas. The first step to improving your emotional adjustment is to recognize the need. Once you realize this, you should ask the Lord to help you with your weaknesses. As you pray and read His Word, you will gain new insights into yourself and the Holy Spirit will lead you into a more effective adjustment. If you feel some special weaknesses which are more serious, you may profit from several counseling sessions with a professionally trained Christian counselor. Everything you do to gain a better level of personal adjustment will make your life fuller and more rewarding as well as adding much strength to your own counseling ministry.

A vital relationship with Jesus Christ is a must for the Christian counselor. If you are going to make a significant and lasting contribution to others, you must communicate the love and reality of the Christian life. Without a vital and growing relationship to the Lord, you will be unable to deal with man's most significant need, the spiritual. As you spend time in His Word and grow closer to the Lord, He will give you fresh lessons and insights which will work miracles in your life and the lives of your counselees.

A sincere interest in others is an essential qualification. Counseling which is done out of a sense of duty rather than a genuine love for others will always be of limited value. People

EMOTIONAL ADJUSTMENT RATING SCALE	Poor	Below Average	Average	Above Average	Excellent
	1	2	3	4	5

I. WHAT KIND OF IMAGE DO I HOLD OF MYSELF?

1. Am I overwhelmed by my own emotions (fears, anger, love, worries, etc.)? . . . .
2. Can I usually take life's disappointments in stride? . .
3. Do I have a tolerant attitude toward myself as well as others? . . . .
4. Can I accept criticism without hostility or hurt? . . .
5. Am I able to gain satisfaction from simple, everyday pleasures? . . . .
6. Do I neither underestimate nor overestimate my abilities?
7. Am I able to accept my own shortcomings? . . . . .
8. Can I take part in many activities with others? . . .
9. Do I have a good measure of self-respect? . . . . .
10. Do I feel able to deal with most situations that come my way? . . . .

II. WHAT ARE MY TRUE FEELINGS ABOUT OTHERS?

1. Am I able to give love to others and consider their interests?
2. Are my personal relationships satisfying and lasting? . .
3. Do I like and trust others, and expect them to like me? .
4. Am I tolerant of others and able to accept our differences?
5. Can I feel I am an accepted member of a group? . .
6. Do I "push" people or allow myself to be pushed around?
7. Can I accept responsibility for my neighbors and friends?

III. HOW DO I MEET THE DEMANDS OF LIFE?

1. Can I do something about my problems as they arise? .
2. Do I accept my just responsibilities? . . . .
3. Can I consider the facts and make mature decisions? .
4. Do I shape and adjust my environment whenever possible?
5. Am I able to plan ahead, but not fear the future? . .
6. Do I welcome new experiences and ideas? . . . . .
7. Am I making use of my natural capacities? . . . . .
8. Do I set realistic goals for myself? . . . .
9. Am I able to think for myself and make my own decisions?
10. Do I put forth my best effort and get satisfaction from it?

Total in each category:

suffering from emotional and spiritual problems are often very sensitive. They are immediately conscious of a shallow and superficial show of interest. They do not respond to the counselor with this attitude. When you have a sincere interest in another person, he senses your love and immediately begins to place his confidence and trust in you. This confidence then becomes the fulcrum of effective counseling.

As a Christian you have a tremendous asset in experiencing a genuine concern for your counselees. Sometimes it is difficult to love a person who seems angry, inconsiderate and ungrateful. Other times you may become frustrated with a counselee because he seems to want to "wallow" in his problems. He may feel sorry for himself, but seemingly refuse to change. In these and similar instances the Lord can give you a heart of real love and concern. We are commanded in the Word to "Be kindly affectioned one to another with brotherly love" (Romans 12:10a), and we are also given the key to this unselfish love. "But the fruit of the Spirit is love, joy, peace, longsuffering, gentleness, goodness, faith, Meekness, temperance: against such there is no law" (Galatians 5:22, 23). God, Himself, is the author of love and only as we walk in close fellowship with Him can we fully experience this affection. As the Holy Spirit controls your life completely, He replaces the concern for *self* with a love for *others*. He removes your impatience, and replaces it with tolerance and concern. He takes an inability to love and substitutes a genuine concern for even the most unlovable. This attitude, imparted to the earnest believer whose life is controlled by the Lord, is the key to a heart and concern for all.

Sensitivity to the needs of others is basic to successful counseling. In addition to a sincere interest in others, you must be alert to people's individual needs. As you sense a problem area or a special sensitivity, you actually communicate to the counselee a feeling of being understood and accepted. If you tell him how he should run his life, you run the risk of breaking down this feeling of mutual understanding and cooperation. Your counselee has had plenty of "advice" and criticism from others. Now he needs sensitive sympathy and understanding. Afterward, he will seek your sincere advice and counsel.

Ability to relate to the counselee's age level is important.

John was an enthusiastic counselor who took an active part in all of the camp recreational activities. He could laugh and joke with the campers but also command their respect. It wasn't long after camp began until several students had come to talk to John about personal problems.

Mary, on the other hand, felt that a lot of the recreation and fun times were "silly and juvenile." She was going to spend her time as a counselor in the most significant way — strictly dealing with important personal matters and spiritual truths. After several days of camp, however, no girls had come to Mary for counseling. Though she had much to offer, the students felt they didn't know her and that she probably didn't "really understand." This matter of personal involvement with young people is tremendously important. Young people go to those with whom they can easily identify. Unless you communicate in some manner your counseling opportunities will be seriously limited.

While it is of utmost importance to relate to the counselee's age level, care must be taken not to remove yourself from a position as a responsible leader. Some counselors err on the side of too complete identification with the counselee. When this happens he is of little value. Young people do not want to take their burdens to another member of the gang. They want to talk with someone they respect as an intelligent, stable and understanding person.

Availability is a key factor in successful counseling. Closely akin to the ability to relate to a counselee is the matter of availability. Some Christian leaders are too busy with planning and programs to find time for individual students. If you expect others to come to you for counsel, you should arrange your schedule so that it is easy for them to contact you and discuss their problems. People suffering from problems frequently fear to seek out a counselor, and they may never come for your assistance unless they know you have the time and interest to see them personally.

The ability to instill confidence in the counselee is an important trait. People beset by problems want to talk to someone who has a positive outlook on life. The counselor who is competent and optimistic in his work soon imparts this same sense of hope and security to his counselee. When a counselor is unsure of his ability and feels there is little chance for progress, he rapidly instills this same feeling into his counselee. Christian counselors here have a tremendous resource, for they rely not alone on their own training and techniques, but most important on the guidance of the Holy Spirit. No matter how new you are to counseling, if you have done your best to prepare by reading and studying appropriate materials, and if you are living close to the Lord, He will give you wisdom and guidance as you deal with others. A tremendous fact in Christian counseling is that it is not merely one person helping another, or even two people working together on a problem. Instead, *it is two people working with the guidance of the Holy Spirit to resolve personal difficulties.* "I can do all things through Christ which strengtheneth me" (Philippians 4:13).

Confidentiality of information is of utmost importance. People want to be especially sure that a counselor is strictly confidential. They want to know that he will not divulge personal information to anyone else.

It is well said that a man's reputation "goes before him." If he is not confidential, the word soon travels, and in a short time people will avoid talking with him about personal matters. It takes only a few "slips" to crystallize an undesirable reputation.

One of the best ways to establish yourself as a dependable counselor is to make sure that what is said to you never goes any further. Even the most gifted counselor will not be sought after if he fails to be confidential. "Confidence in an unfaithful man in time of trouble is like a broken tooth, and a foot out of joint" (Proverbs 25:19). People refuse to take chances on what they consider "private affairs." So if you would have people turn to you, be sure you guard their confidences.

Every counselor enters the counseling relationship at different levels of adjustment on the attitudes and concepts discussed above. If you naturally have many of these strengths you are well along the road to successful counseling experiences. If you feel you do not measure up to these standards, do not lose heart and interest in counseling. The Lord has the power to promote growth and Christian character in you, and He wants to do this in your life. So set out a path of greater yieldedness and sensitivity to His guidance. As you earnestly turn to Him in prayer and study, He will produce in you a strong and mature Christian character which can be used mightily for His honor and glory.

Questions for Discussion

1. Why is a counselor's own adjustment important in counseling?
2. How can a counselor improve his adjustment?
3. How might a counselor project his own problems on to the person he is counseling?
4. What is the significance of a counselor talking about his own experiences?
5. List some characteristics of a well-adjusted person.
6. What is meant by one's self-image or self-concept?
7. How does a person develop the image which he holds of himself?
8. How does a person develop his basic feelings about people?
9. List three reasons why a person may find it difficult to invest himself freely in others.
10. Why are some people unable to develop realistic goals for themselves?
11. Why do some people find it difficult to make decisions?
12. Why might a person find it difficult to genuinely compliment others?
13. How can a counselor communicate the fact that God loves and cares for a counselee?
14. Why are people with emotional and spiritual problems often very sensitive?
15. What is meant by the statement, "God is the author of love"?
16. How can a counselor gain the confidence of those with whom he counsels?
17. Why do some counselors find it difficult to be confidential?
18. How can a counselor become more yielded to Christ?
19. Can a counselor help a counselee to surrender to Christ if the counselor, himself, has areas of reservation?
20. What insights into your own personality have you gained through this chapter?

4

Understanding Children and Youth

THE STUDY OF human behavior is fascinating. Every person is different — and worth understanding. Some behavior is obvious; other is puzzling. This is especially true of young people. Never in life is the unexpected so normal as in youth. Personalities are forming. Relationships are growing. Values are being considered and a personal relationship to Jesus Christ is often established.

Let's consider now some of the premises basic to the understanding of human behavior:

ALL BEHAVIOR IS CAUSED

Human actions are not merely chance occurrences. There are reasons why people act as they do. One person reacts to frustrations with feelings of worthlessness and self-blame. Another expresses strong resentment and hostility. Is this chance? Are some of us "just made that way"? No, there are reasons for these responses. Aunt Mary is not just naturally nosy and interfering. Rebellious Jim didn't just happen to lose his temper. John did not accidentally ask Christ to come into his life and save him. There is a history of experience behind the action we observe.

CAUSES ARE MULTIPLE

Human behavior does not occur in isolation. The way we feel and react in one area of life influences the whole person. The three circles on page 28 illustrate this principle of multiple causation.

The psalmist says we are "fearfully and wonderfully made" (Psalm 139:14). In I Thessalonians 5:23 we read "And the very God of peace sanctify you wholly; and I pray God your whole *spirit* and *soul* and *body* be preserved blameless unto the coming of our Lord Jesus Christ." The spiritual realm of man is that part which enables us to relate to and understand the communi-

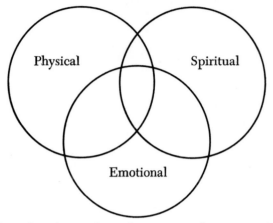

cation of God. The soul is the center of our emotions and
attitudes and our self-consciousness. Through our physical
bodies we relate to the world about us through the five senses.

Each of these areas overlap and interrelate. When a person
is suffering much physical pain and fatigue his emotions are
also affected. When experiencing feelings of emotional depression and discouragement, it is extremely difficult to maintain
proper lines of spiritual communication. When a Christian is out
of fellowship with the Lord, he is much more susceptible to emotional conflicts and frustrations. These three aspects of man
cannot be delineated or separated. What happens in one
intimately influences every other area. In order to understand
human behavior we must be aware of this concept. We are not
recognizing the whole person when we tell a person with a
severe physical or emotional problem to go home and pray and
read his Bible. The problem may not be spiritual, but rather,
emotional. On the other hand we are not effective if we treat
a spiritual difficulty as if it were an emotional disturbance.
You can counsel for months with no significant progress if you
neglect to deal with your counselee's personal relationship to
Jesus Christ. And in some instances a hidden physical problem
such as a glandular imbalance or a neurological impairment may
give symptoms which appear to be primarily spiritual or emotional. A thyroid deficiency, for example, may bring a slowing
of bodily processes, feelings of fatigue, depression and over-
weight. If this malfunctioning is not corrected, even a great

amount of spiritual and emotional counseling will be of little avail.

With every counselee, one of your first tasks is to determine the basic causal factors. Is this behavior caused by the natural inclinations of the unsaved? Is it due to emotional factors lying in childhood experiences? Or is it basically a physical disturbance? Only after a correct initial evaluation will you be able to deal properly with a person.

Behavior derives from basic motivations. Behind all behavior are certain motivating forces. The crying infant is communicating his need for food or physical comfort. The teen-ager often tries to attend a multitude of social functions in an attempt to fulfill a basic need for acceptance. The native hunter in the jungle of South America may be striving to meet certain physical and social drives. The status-conscious young businessman is sometimes driven to long labors because he wants to "get ahead" in life.

Every human organism is motivated by a number of internal and external forces. The most basic of these are the physical. Human beings must satisfy their needs for food and shelter before they can expend energy in search of emotional gratifications. Sexual drives are also strongly physically based and are important determinants of behavior. If you are to understand human behavior you must ask the question, "What is the motivating force behind this action?" "What need is this person trying to fill by his actions?" When these questions are answered, you are well on your way to a thorough understanding of the problem.

After a person has developed adequate resources for meeting his *basic physical wants,* he can turn to the satisfaction of various emotional needs. These needs may not overtly appear as strong as physical motivators, but they are extremely important. A great portion of human energy is devoted to satisfying these basic emotional wants.

Every person needs *the assurance that he belongs* — that he is desired, and that in his absence he is missed. This is one of man's basic emotional needs. The search for belongingness motivates much of human behavior.

Individuals also need to feel they are achieving and being successful. When a person is a constant failure, he develops feelings of inadequacy and unworthiness. Every human being is motivated by a search for a sense of achievement and adequacy.

Young people need to be relatively *free from fear.* All people strive toward a level of inner confidence which frees them from distressing anxiety and fear. As you study behavior you will find that many people are reacting basically in an attempt to avoid or overcome these feelings of apprehension and fear.

People of all ages need much *love and affection.* They not only need to be loved; they need to be told that they are loved. When love is not there, youngsters often turn to deviant means of finding acceptance. The rebellious adolescent delinquent, for example, may be motivated by a search for attention he did not receive from his parents. His actions may also be a retaliation against those who failed to give him needed love and affection. Every one of us is strongly motivated by this need for acceptance.

Freedom from feelings of guilt and blame is another goal of much human behavior. People want to feel worthy and adequate. The person who is preoccupied with feelings of guilt and sinfulness is unhappy and maladjusted. One of the strongest motivating forces in his life is the search for freedom from the binding influences of these feelings.

The greatest need of every individual is to have *an abiding faith in God.* Human beings are spiritual beings and their personalities are never fully developed unless they have many experiences which develop their faith. The search for meaning and purpose in life through faith in Jesus Christ is a prime motivating force in human adjustment. God has created human beings in His own likeness. And as spiritual beings with a capacity for God, they are never satisfied until they have a personal relationship with their Maker.

These are some of the most important of man's physical, emotional and spiritual needs. An understanding of the influence of these various motivating factors holds the key to the proper understanding of those with whom you counsel.

An individual's behavior is his best attempt to reach an acceptable level of adjustment. No matter how "good" or how "bad" a person's behavior may seem, it is serving a useful purpose in his life. People don't want to be unhappy and disturbed — they seek the most satisfactory level of adjustment possible. Rebellious Jim is not just trying to make everyone miserable; he gets some satisfaction from this. The depression of a middle-aged mother is her best attempt to cope with problems. At every turn over the years she made the choices and attitudes she felt would best protect her identity and adjustment. She took each path because it seemed less harmful and threatening than another. It is sometimes difficult to understand what value maladjustive behavior has, but as we begin to fully understand the causes it becomes clear that this path of adjustment has been the one which appeared (consciously or unconsciously) to hold the most effective adjustment. With counseling, however, these individuals can begin to learn new ways of behaving which are more effective and satisfying. This is the task of the counselor — to help people overcome these old habits and maladaptive patterns of reaction and to replace them with more wholesome and gratifying means of behaving.

The source of current problems may be found in present or past experiences. John's father had recently been severely injured in an automobile accident. John had to drop out of all extra school activities so he could help support the family. He came to his pastor quite discouraged. He was suffering from some feelings of depression; he felt he was losing interest in spiritual matters and his school work was falling down. In John's case the major causes of his problem were recent and situational.

On the other hand, Mary came to her youth leader with very similar feelings. She was discouraged and depressed and was losing interest in spiritual things. She said that God felt far away and she knew He couldn't really be interested in her. During a number of visits with her youth leader, it became apparent that Mary's problem had deep roots. Her mother worked when Mary was young and spent little time alone with her. The father's work involved much traveling, and he was often out of town on business. When home he showed little interest in either Mary or her younger brother. Discipline was often harsh and Mary had no one to understand her — no one to whom she could turn. These childhood experiences had

caused her to feel inadequate and unworthy. Now she was
feeling depressed and discouraged. She found it hard to understand God's love and forgiveness since she had not experienced
this from her earthly parents. Her problems did *not* lie in
present circumstances like John's. Mary had deeper problems
which took several months to resolve.

People respond to understanding. Many people go through
life maladjusted because no one has taken sufficient time to try
to understand them. Even the most unloving and resentful
person has an underlying desire to be accepted and loved. On
the outside he may seem rough and resistant to all overtures of
sympathy. Deep within, however, lies a strong need to be
understood. It is the maladjusted person who is usually most
difficult to love. It is with the person who is rebellious
and hostile toward God that we frequently lose patience. But
these are just the ones who need calm acceptance and understanding. It may take much time but you can usually win them
over with an earnest concern. With an understanding of this
principle you can be more tolerant to those who seemingly turn
away from help.

Now that we have considered some basic principles of human
behavior, let us turn to the major characteristics of young people.

Human beings are characterized by change and dynamic.
The child of six, for example, is quite different from the child
of four. In two years' time many changes have taken place in
his physical, emotional and spiritual adjustment. And so it is
with all ages. A girl reacts differently at fifteen than she will at
twenty. Her basic needs remain the same, but many significant
changes have taken place. If we are to work effectively with
young people, we must have a basic understanding of the more
important characteristics of different age levels.

DEVELOPMENTAL FACTORS

Growing children and youth are changing rapidly and
significantly from year to year. One of the most important areas
of knowledge for all who are working with this age group is
the changing characteristics of youth. It is not enough to say,
"This child is young; therefore he is immature and needs much
guidance." The average eight-year-old shows different physical

and emotional characteristics than the ten-year-old. In order to better understand the adjustment problems of youth you need to know what is normal behavior for various age levels. It is not significant to say of a six-year-old, "He is extremely impulsive." That is normal! But if you make the same statement about a college sophomore, you are communicating meaningful data. To say that a teen-ager is having trouble getting along with his parents is not necessarily significant. Most adolescents have some trouble in this area. But when a seven-year-old is already showing strong hostility and rebellion, he is exhibiting unexpected and abnormal characteristics.

Human behavior can be studied from many angles. One of the most basic of these is the concept of dependency. Each person strives to grow from the total dependency of infancy to a mature and self-reliant independence. This struggle from dependence to self-reliance does not come easily. It is a gradual process of growth. Notice, for example, the three age groups discussed in this volume from the standpoint of striving toward independence.

The child from six to nine is basically dependent. He is beginning to establish relationships outside of the home, but still finds most of his emotional and physical needs met by his parents. This child recognizes his dependence upon others and does not hesitate to admit it. When he has a need it is taken to Mom or Dad. This is the normal process for him. He is not yet old enough to stand alone and is grateful for the opportunity to turn to others for support and guidance.

The preadolescent (9-12) is another step along the road to maturity. He has developed greater abilities than the younger child and is able to satisfy some of his own needs. In some cases he is already partially responsible for earning a living. This age child is a person in conflict. Unlike the younger child, the preadolescent may not readily admit his needs for dependency. Since he has greater resources for meeting the needs of life, he desires independence and freedom. The bounds of parental authority become frustrating. At one minute he wants to prove that he can do things on his own. He may resent interference and direction. He is striving to demonstrate his individuality. But in another moment he turns for support and guidance. Now he wants the reassurance and comfort of adults. He knows he needs help in meeting the problems of life. So he is frustrated. First he wants to go it alone, then he turns for aid. This is the world of the preadolescent. In times of independence he needs your support and encouragement to reach out on his own. In times of need he wants your quiet assurance and gentle direction.

During the teen years a boy or girl becomes more independent. To a much greater degree than the preadolescent, there is less need of parental authority and control. The young person wants to prove his maturity and he needs the opportunity. He does not want constant supervision and direction. He needs to make mistakes and to learn. By late teen years most people have basically reached their limits of physical and mental development. They have the capacity but are short on experience. They need and desire the opportunity to take responsibility, but there are still some needs for dependency. The young person is still financially dependent and his emotions are unstable. He needs guidance and direction but will not usually accept it when given in a domineering and authoritative manner. He wants to know where he can come for assistance, but he does not want to be told he needs it. When he is ready he will come.

When behavior is evaluated in the frame of reference of this process of growing independence, it is more easily understood. The young child can be seen as an integral part of a dependent family relationship. The preadolescent is starting to break these ties. He has an ambivalent attitude toward his own dependency needs. To the teen-ager the struggle toward self-direction is one of the most necessary and important goals of life.

And on the process goes — never completed but always moving forward. By realizing this striving from dependence to self-reliance you better understand the dynamics of human behavior. When a young child has a problem, you can realize there is little you can do with him alone unless you are assuming (perhaps temporarily) a parental or authority figure role.

If you are a teacher, a camp counselor or someone who is responsible for a child, you can talk with him and learn more of his problems. Then you can encourage him to talk, encourage him generally, lead him close to Christ, and in many other ways assist him.

With the preadolescent you definitely see the value of private counsel — not extensively, but in many ways. The eleven-year-old can greatly profit from wise counsel. He has many questions and conflicts. You can be a great blessing by helping him to evaluate many daily decisions and lead him into a closer relationship with Christ. But because he is still dependent, long-term counseling should involve parents to help them gain insight into the problem. A combination of efforts is most effective for this age.

As a young person approaches adulthood, he is more able to stand on his own and take full responsibility for his actions. Your counseling with this age can be devoted primarily to the counselee. It is often good to bring the parents into the counseling relationship, but this is not always needed. The young person is mature enough to face clearly his relationship to Jesus Christ! He has a well-developed sense of morality and justice and knows the consequences of his actions. The ability to take responsibility for his actions is present. Because of this you can have a tremendous influence, assisting in his further steps to maturity. Your counseling ministry can have deep and lasting value.

Having looked at the basic concept of growing toward maturity and independence, let us consider some of the basic physical and emotional characteristics of various age levels. A knowledge of these characteristics and interests will help you understand boys and girls better.

CHILDREN (ages approximately six to nine)

Physical and Emotional Characteristics
1. Growth slowing down
2. Large muscles better developed than small ones
3. Tremendous energy but easily fatigued
4. Impulsive, especially at younger ages
5. Unable to maintain long attention span
6. Family ties are first separated to allow school relationships
7. Lessening dependence on mother

8. Not discriminating with reference to social position, race or religion
9. Conscience and sense of morality is developing rapidly
10. Frequently careless and untidy
11. Developing understanding of concepts of time, money and distance
12. Beginning to develop abstract thinking ability
13. Greater desire for freedom
14. Very little concern over the future
15. Acquiring basic intellectual skills such as reading and writing

Interests and Needs

1. Some independence and some encouraging support
2. Learning situations with concrete objects
3. Warmth and encouragement from adults
4. Broadening experiences to satisfy growing interests
5. Physical activity
6. Considerate answers to questions concerning coming physiological changes
7. Opportunities to discuss respect for property, respect for others
8. Reasonable explanations
9. Opportunity for committee work, construction and dramatic work.
10. Some quiet activities
11. Belonging to a group of children of same age
12. Parent or older adult of same sex to identify with

PREADOLESCENTS (approximately ten to thirteen)

Physical and Emotional Characteristics

1. Steady growth during first portion with rapid growth common at 12 or 13
2. Marked differences in size at this age
3. Girls commonly larger than boys
4. Onset of secondary sex characteristics
5. Girls expected to mature one or two years earlier than boys
6. Interested in gangs, clubs and teams

7. Scornful of opposite sex, with girls breaking out of this pattern sooner
8. Having a strong sense of justice
9. May be untidy
10. Much energy and daring
11. Able to concentrate for longer periods
12. Greater tendency to separate work from play
13. Hands and feet may seem unproportionately large
14. Desirous of group approval
15. Rather self-conscious about participating in physical activity unless skilled
16. Tendency toward awkwardness, poor posture and laziness
17. Boys and girls teasing each other
18. Transition from childhood to adolescence
19. Developing ability to postpone satisfactions
20. Increased awareness of own assets and liabilities
21. Voice changes may begin in boys
22. Broadening interests
23. Friendships become more stable and lasting
24. Sense of humor developing

Interests and Needs

1. Inclusion in family and school planning
2. Knowledge regarding maturational differences between boys and girls
3. Some close friends
4. Recognition for efforts put forth
5. Opportunity to make some decisions
6. Girls need knowledge regarding approaching menstruation
7. A place where privacy and possessions are respected
8. Opportunity to earn and spend money
9. Social activities for both boys and girls
10. Challenging activities that foster spiritual growth
11. Understanding of physical and emotional changes which have come or are about to come
12. Adults in whom to confide
13. Intellectual challenges at own level

YOUNG PEOPLE (high school and college)

Physical and Emotional Characteristics

1. Sexual maturation, with accompanying physical and emotional changes
2. Early awkward period followed by development of grace and coordination
3. Increase in muscular strength
4. Desiring age group approval more than parent or adult approval
5. Evidencing pronounced individual differences
6. Marked instability gradually replaced as adulthood nears
7. Wanting to earn wages
8. Girls desiring to be "pretty"
9. Boys desiring to be strong and healthy
10. Evidencing considerable idealism
11. Seeking independence
12. Developing social abilities
13. Family relationships may be strained
14. Interested in opposite sex: prone to temporary "crushes"
15. Going to extremes with occasional "know it all" attitude
16. Seeking adult equality
17. Interested in establishing a philosophy of life
18. Preoccupied with acceptance by the group
19. Identifying closely with an admired adult, idolizing some hero
20. Concerned over spiritual issues and destiny

Interests and Needs

1. Adequate physical appearance
2. Acceptance by the peer group
3. Guidance which is kindly, unobtrusive and does not threaten the young person's feeling of freedom
4. Vocational direction
5. Knowledge and understanding of wholesome sex relationships and attitudes
6. Assurance of security
7. Independence
8. Provision for constructive recreation

9. Strong family solidarity in a new world of widened opportunities and confusion
10. Wholesome activities for boundless energy
11. Encouragement in experiences which will develop an abiding religious faith
12. Opportunities for creative activities
13. Opportunity to increase in knowledge

From the foregoing characteristics you can see that all children and young people are passing through developmental stages. They all go through the same stages, *but not at the same age nor at the same rate.* Therefore, a child of eight may still be working on a certain development that another child of six or seven is. Also, a boy of seventeen may still be struggling with a developmental factor that another boy of fifteen has already accomplished. The wise counselor, therefore, will consider the behavior of children and young people from a developmental point of view, asking himself, "Why is he acting the way he is? What is he working on? What is he trying to tell me? How can I best help him?"

QUESTIONS FOR DISCUSSION

1. What is the significance of the statement, "All behavior is caused"?
2. Why are causes of problems generally multiple?
3. Why are physical, spiritual and emotional causes often interrelated?
4. How might a physical problem affect a person spiritually?
5. How might feelings of depression affect a person's attitude toward God?
6. How might a lack of spiritual dedication affect a person emotionally?
7. What is meant by motivating forces?
8. How might a person act if he feels he is not accepted?
9. What would cause a person to feel that he does not belong?
10. How might a series of successful experiences affect a person?
11. How might a series of failures affect a person?
12. Why is love and affection so important to a child?

13. How might feelings of constant fear in childhood affect a person later in life?

14. Why does a person long to be free from feelings of guilt?

15. What kinds of experiences other than the transgression of God's laws might cause a person to feel unworthy and guilty?

16. Why is a person's abiding faith in God, through Christ, his greatest need?

17. Discuss the following statement: "An individual's behavior is his attempt to achieve an acceptable level of adjustment."

18. How might a person's current problems be found in either his present or past experiences?

19. What are some ways in which a counselor can communicate to a counselee that the counselor does understand?

20. What is meant by developmental factors?

21. Do all children and youth pass through the same developmental stages at the same time? Explain.

22. What could be the significance of two adolescents, one fourteen and another seventeen, demonstrating the same level of emotional development?

23. Discuss a child or young person's striving to become independent.

24. When working with a child, why is it important to counsel with his parents?

25. Summarize what you have learned in this chapter about developmental factors.

5

Techniques of Counseling

EVERY PROFESSION is characterized by its own techniques and skills. Mathematicians, for example, follow certain procedures. Astronomers have their specialized ways of working. Medical doctors adhere closely to specific routines. And so it is with all scientifically-trained groups.

Professional counselors, too, have developed certain techniques which enable them to work effectively with people. Whether you spend much or just a limited amount of time counseling, you will benefit from knowing as much as possible about professional techniques. Even though your counseling may be informal with only brief and limited contacts, you should develop as much insight as you can, then work at the level which is appropriate for you.

All counselors can steadily improve their counseling ability. Some need to develop emotionally themselves. Many can profit from further study of human development. Nearly all have strong needs for improved techniques of counseling. One of the most difficult tasks of an inexperienced counselor is to understand the general process of therapy. But without this knowledge much time and effectiveness is lost. In this section we will consider *the stages of counseling,* and some of the most basic and important *counseling techniques.*

In some settings you are limited to three or four contacts with a counselee. Even in this short time you can accomplish much if the problem is not severe. When faced with such a time limitation you can keep three goals in mind.

First, assist the counselee to develop all possible insights into his problem. Help him to consider the emotional and spiritual aspects and to seek the influence of past relationships and events to the current problem.

A *second* goal is to lead the counselee into a deeper relationship with Christ so he can turn to the Word of God for continued strength and guidance. Many problems are basically emotional, in many others the difficulty is mostly spiritual. One of the greatest challenges as a counselor is to help a young person come to a saving knowledge of Jesus Christ, then to dedicate his life entirely to the Lord. *Failure to surrender to the sovereignty of God is the basic cause of many problems.*

The *third* major goal of short-term counseling is to encourage the young person to seek further counsel, if needed. He might profit from several discussions with a minister or youth leader. If the problem is obviously a serious emotional difficulty, you can encourage professional help from a counselor or psychologist. Many young people feel anxious or embarrassed about going to a professional counselor, so you help them immeasurably by explaining the value of such therapy.

The broad outline of the counseling process presented below *applies basically to more serious problems.* But it can also serve as a guide in situations when you have only three or four counseling sessions and you are handling less serious problems.

Stages of Counseling

The beginning stage of counseling usually consists of from one to several interviews. The first goal of this stage is to establish a good relationship. Without an attitude of mutual trust and acceptance the counseling process cannot continue beyond this first phase. The first one or two sessions are very important. In these interviews the heart of the real problem is seldom touched, but this is desirable. People do not like to share serious conflicts and burdens with a stranger. It takes time to develop confidence. By working too fast and asking probing questions too early, you may frighten your counselee away or cause him to be on guard against your prying. He will bring up disturbing points when he feels at ease with you.

Nearly every counselee brings a pseudo problem to the first interview. It is often of a situational nature. Mary, for example, brought the following problem to her youth minister: "I really love to be with our high school gang on the gospel team, but I'm just too scared to even give a testimony." Her wise pastor realized that Mary's problem could simply be inexperience, or, lack of spiritual dedication. He also wondered if this might represent a more serious problem. As they talked together for several sessions, it became obvious that Mary's problem was not a fear of witnessing. Actually, *she was very insecure and fearful in all social situations.* By working on this underlying problem they were able not only to remove her fear of witnessing, but also to improve her total personality adjustment. She gradually began to emerge from a shell of quietness into a more active and happy person. She had more confidence at home, at school and at church. If her pastor had accepted at face value the original statement, he would have missed Mary's real problem. This presenting a pseudo problem is a characteristic of the beginning stage of therapy.

During *the initial phase of counseling* you should make a tentative diagnosis or judgment of the problem. You can ask yourself questions such as, "What is the *real* problem?" "Is this a temporary situational disturbance or something more severe and complex?" "Is this basically a spiritual problem or does it have emotional and physical aspects?" "Am I qualified to handle this or should I refer to someone better trained?" "Is this a problem that can be resolved in a few sessions or should we have appointments for a longer period of time?" "Do I need to get outside help from parents, school or church?" "What are the major causes of the problem?" Without an understanding of these questions you will wander aimlessly through a maze of seemingly unrelated discussion and emotion. With these questions tentatively answered you are in a position to begin a serious effort to resolve the problem.

Another major goal of the initial stage of therapy is to structure the counseling process. Most young people feel they can talk to you for one or two hours and resolve their problems. They expect quick answers. One of your first responsibilities is to help them understand that most problems are years in developing and require much time to resolve. You can also utilize this time to explain a little about the nature of problems. Show your counselee that most problems have both spiritual and emotional aspects, and indicate that you will want to consider both of these. Assure him that all discussion will be kept confidential and that you want to work together with him in resolving the difficulty. This initial structuring sets the stage for an organized and effective counseling process.

Some time after the first few interviews you enter into *the second phase of counseling*. You have structured the interview and the counselee is relating well. He trusts you and is feeling free to share more personal thoughts. You have evaluated the presenting problem and looked for the more basic conflicts. A tentative diagnosis of the type and severity of the problem has been made, and you have an idea of the help which would best resolve the conflict.

Now you begin to reach the heart of the problem. As the actual conflict approaches, tears may come. The counselee may find it more difficult to talk. He may try to avoid the problem. This is when you need to be exceptionally understanding and accepting. By gently encouraging expression of true feelings, you make it easier for the counselee to discuss disturbing conflicts. As the heart of the problem is touched, you enter into the most significant phase of counseling. The problem is ventilated; it is accepted; the causes are identified; its effects are discussed and the means of overcoming it are gradually focused upon. Only with such a thorough process can deep-seated problems be permanently overcome. The key word to this second stage of therapy is *insight*. It is here that the counselee gains a true understanding of the problem, its causes and effects and the cure. This most significant aspect of therapy is the longest phase. In minor problems only a few sessions may be required. In more serious difficulties counseling may last for many weeks or months. In any instance, this period should not be rushed. It is the crux of successful counseling.

After the problem has been worked through in detail, *the final stage of counseling* is reached. The key to this phase of therapy is independence and self-direction. While in the former sessions the counselee may have been dependent on your support, encouragement and assistance, he must now learn to accept full responsibility for his adjustment. In less serious problems this stage is very easy and, indeed, sometimes unnecessary. But with long-term counseling a gradual process of weaning may be indicated. Instead of weekly sessions the counselee may begin to come every other week until he is gradually terminated. With a growing independence and self-reliance, the counselee will be able to handle future conflicts without turning to others for assistance.

The Counseling Process

Having considered the broad outline of stages of therapy, we will now turn to some specific techniques and concepts in the counseling process.

Be Prepared

Sometimes a young person brings a problem to you unexpectedly. Often, however, you have access to helpful information before your first actual counseling session. When this occurs you should consider several things. The most basic preparation is your personal attitude and a time in prayer for guidance and understanding. Following this you should consider certain information about your counselee. Does he know Christ as his personal Savior? Is he a member of a Bible-believing church? Is he a socially active person or more quiet and withdrawn? Are there obvious evidences of emotional or spiritual problems? What about his parents? Are they believers? Do they have a happy home life? What are his brothers and sisters like? Do they, too, evidence adjustment difficulties? These and other questions are very important. If you know the answers to some of them, you will be much more effective during the actual counseling time.

Be a Good Listener

Every person wants to feel wanted and important. One of the most effective ways to communicate your interest to a counselee is to listen intently to what he says. By giving your undivided attention, you are saying that he is important to you and that you earnestly share his burden. As one girl said of a youth counselor, "He's the first person who ever listened to what I had to say."

Even when a person speaks of seemingly irrelevant experiences, you should be listening for significant cues. Important data is often revealed through seemingly trivial experiences.

There's an old saying: "Friends listen, but enemies talk." And this is basically true. As you hear a person out, you not only recognize his worth; you also promote significant insights.

Make Your Counseling a Process, Not a Lecture

One of the most difficult concepts for young counselors to understand is the fact that counseling takes time. It is the natural thing to listen to a problem for a few minutes then begin to give advice. It is difficult to restrain yourself — to take time to fully explore and resolve a conflict. If problems have been several years in formation, they usually cannot be solved in one session of counseling. The roots are deep and must be slowly uncovered, evaluated and overcome. When a person brings an obviously serious problem you should suggest that several periods be set aside to discuss the situation fully. This gives time for a more thorough discussion and avoids superficial treatment of serious disturbances.

Encourage Complete Discussion

Every problem has many ramifications and needs thorough discussion in order to gain a full understanding. In trying to save time, an inexperienced counselor may encourage the counselee to discuss only a few basic areas of conflict. Sometimes this is necessary because of limited time. On the other hand, if full benefit is to be derived from counseling, all related areas must be explored. Nothing the counselee says is unimportant. There is a reason for nearly every word he says, and an understanding of why he speaks the words he does gives greater insight into his total adjustment. People need an opportunity to express the emotional reactions they have had to various people and experiences. They need to evaluate these. Frequently this takes a number of counseling sessions, but it is such thoroughness that brings lasting results.

As a counselee discusses his problems, he may mention the same set of experiences over and over again. For example, a troubled girl may talk about her relationship with her mother not just once, but many times. She may continue to repeat the same episodes, thus giving her relief and bringing deeper insights. The effective counselor recognizes the value of such re-

When should one begin opening into solution?

peated discussions. The inexperienced counselor tends to bypass this process. He may "see" the causes, then quickly tell the person what is wrong with him and what he should do about it.

But such procedures are rarely helpful. They may only frustrate the troubled person and cause him to feel rejected. The wise counselor, therefore, will encourage the counselee to discuss this problem fully.

Accept the Counselee As a Worthy Person

The core of many emotional problems lies in feelings of unworthiness and inadequacy. You, as a counselor, are often the first person to really accept your counselee without criticism or condition. Whereas parents or others may have accepted him only when he was obedient or successful, *you have an opportunity to demonstrate God's unconditional acceptance.* When a person feels unworthy and inadequate he cannot function well. When a child's parents show love and acceptance only for desirable behavior, the child constantly fears rejection and rebuff. Since earthly parents may have shown love only when he was good, the child feels that God also can only love those who are "worthy." This attitude is a severe detriment to spiritual growth. But when you begin to accept your counselee at all times, even when he expresses negative feelings, you are telling him that love need not be conditional. You are saying that you respect him in spite of his behavior. You are vividly portraying the fact that God can hate *sin*, but at the very moment love the *sinner*. This often is a difficult balance to strike. When you have high moral and spiritual standards, it is natural to want others to share them and to condemn anything less. It is important that you avoid this. One way to overcome your tendency to condemn is to remember your counselee earnestly in prayer. If there is sin in his life, ask the Holy Spirit to convict. Your counselee is usually well-aware of sin, and your pointing critically to it may set a barrier between you. Sin, of course, is a reality and it must be dealt with in a real way. It is to be detected, confessed, and forgiven by God. Dealing with sin directly is a must in many cases. However, exercise must be taken not to reject the counselee at the same time you point out that God rejects his sinful practices.

Another way of dealing with unacceptable behavior without

criticism is to encourage the counselee to discuss his own feelings about his behavior. Since he generally knows the implications of sin, he will usually talk about his guilt and make confession to the Lord if he is encouraged to discuss his feelings.

A third way of dealing with sin without overt condemnation is to share a portion of scripture. Rather than proudly displaying a verse to prove a point, you might ask him to read a passage and tell you what he thinks it means. The Word will speak for itself in conviction and you will not be seen as another judgmental authority figure.

Complete respect for a counselee as a worthy person must be communicated throughout each interview, not alone when dealing with some obvious sin. Feelings of inadequacy or inferiority often cause a person to feel just as rejected and condemned as criticism for sin. Thus you need to communicate the fact that you think he is a worthy person in spite of his feelings of inadequacy. Through speech and through silence you can express this attitude of respect and esteem for your counselee. As you do he can slowly begin to experience this acceptance of you and thereby develop a relationship in which you can help him.

Don't Be Shocked

Martha came to her camp counselor with a serious problem concerning her sexual adjustment.

"Martha," exclaimed her counselor. "Not you!"

Any possible progress in counseling was blocked immediately. The counselor's reaction of shock made the young girl feel that she was being condemned again, and that her counselor really didn't understand. Some people feel that by expressing shock and disappointment, they can shame the counselee into change. But such is not the case. When a person has a problem, he needs to know that he is accepted. He also needs to realize that "the world will not come to an end because of one difficulty" and that others have similar problems. By communicating an optimistic attitude of acceptance you instill in the counselee a sense of understanding as well as a new hope and confidence that the problem can be understood and resolved.

Any expression of alarm will usually seriously hinder an effective counseling relationship.

Use Open End Questions

A very simple but often neglected technique of counseling is to phrase questions so that the counselee must answer with some discussion rather than a "yes" or "no." If you ask "Do you feel your mother is part of this problem?" your counselee may reply, "No." If you say, "What are some of the ways your mother has influenced your feelings?" he will be encouraged to think of a number of possibilities. Questions that can be answered with a single word should be avoided. They can quickly turn a counseling interview into a question and answer period.

Don't Be an Answer Man

Most people come to a counselor seeking answers. They want to pose a question and get immediate solutions. You should usually avoid giving a direct answer to a question until you fully understand the reason behind it. Jane, for example, went to a youth counselor with the following question: "Do you think it is wrong for a Christian to dance?" Without thinking the question through, her counselor quickly replied in the affirmative. Jane asked a few more questions on why dancing was not appropriate for Christians and then ended the conversation. Was Jane really asking if dancing was appropriate? Or was she thinking of a greater issue: separation and dedication? Perhaps she was having a serious conflict with her parents over this question. Was hers basically a spiritual problem? Because a rapid answer was given, this counselor failed to solve the basic problem. Had the counselor encouraged Jane by asking, "What do you think about it?" or "What do most of your friends think?" she would have opened the door for a more thorough discussion of the real issue. So beware of giving short, pat answers. When someone asks you a direct question, try to turn the question back to him and encourage throughtful discussion of the problem.

Avoiding direct questions does not mean that you never answer a counselee. On the contrary, you have much knowledge and maturity from which he can profit. The problem is not whether to answer a question, but rather, *how and when to respond.* Any time a counselee can come to his own Biblical decision, you usually do a disservice by providing him your answer. Your goal should always be to help the counselee develop insight and maturity so that he can reach his own decisions based upon the Word of God.

Don't Overestimate the Problem

There is a delicate balance in evaluating the severity of any problem. Some professional people tend to make a severe personality disturbance out of a minor maladjustment. Lay people, on the other hand, are frequently prone to dismiss even quite serious problems as normal. Rebellious "teen-age" Bob might be considered a sociopathic personality by the local psychologist, a spiritual rebel by his minister and a kid "just feeling his oats" by his friends. There is a balance between these which varies with the problem. One of your first duties as a counselor is to recognize the severity of a problem. Many people today are carrying unnecessary conflicts and maladjustments because years ago someone minimized the problem and suggested that no help was needed. If you do this you may be partially responsible for a failure to obtain needed professional assistance. When a person has a broken leg, we do not suggest it is probably only a sprain. We immediately suggest the needed professional diagnosis and treatment. The same is true of emotional disturbances.

At the same time, you do not want to make every minor maladjustment appear as a severe problem. By doing so you may frighten a counselee and cause him to lose faith in your ability. Only as you strike a reasonable balance between these two extremes can you be most effective. If you overestimate a problem you may threaten the counselee and waste unnecessary energy. If you underestimate the disturbance you will give only superficial and temporary assistance.

Reflect His Statements

A simple but basic technique of counseling is to reflect the counselee's feelings. This encourages him to talk more and it also tells him that you do understand how he feels. If a counselee makes a statement such as, "Bob sure makes me mad!" you may reflect his feelings by saying "He really rubs you the wrong way." As you reply in this manner your counselee senses that you understand. Because you reflected his statement, he is likely to express himself more fully. This is the key to both of you gaining a deeper understanding of the actual problem.

Clarify His Feelings

People with emotional problems frequently do not understand their own feelings. Because they are so involved, they are unable to look objectively and gain a realistic understanding of their attitudes. One of the most important duties will be to clarify these confused feelings.

Example of a counselor helping to restate and clarify the counselee's feelings:

Counselee: "I don't really like to join in many activities."

Counselor: "You prefer to stay at home alone."

Counselee: "Not at home necessarily . . . I just don't like to be with a lot of people. Like when the kids go out for a coke after a game. I would just as soon go home."

Counselor: "Sometimes you feel uneasy when you are with a group."

Counselee: "I guess so. I just don't feel a part of the group."

Counselor: "You mean you feel that no one is interested in you?"

Counselee: "Yes, its that way all the time. I'm never a part of the gang at school. And at church I never seem to make many friends. Even when I sit in a big group it seems like I'm all alone."

The counselee began with the statement, "I don't really like to join in many activities," but was led by the counselor to express the fact that she felt lonely and rejected and wasn't able to make friends. The counselee was beginning to expand her thinking and get more thoughts out in the open where they could be evaluated and understood. This process gradually leads to greater insight and understanding into one's feelings and emotions. Without this, no real solution to the problem can be found.

Listen for Themes

In every counseling experience many different topics are discussed. Some are obviously important and others seem of little significance. Throughout them all one or two basic streams of thought may usually be detected.

For example, Bob was from a divorced home. He was talking to a school counselor about some problems. During this time he mentioned getting kicked off the football team for staying out beyond curfew. This was very upsetting to him since football was an important part of his high school life. Bob also mentioned a recent rift with his girl. Later on he told how badly he felt when criticized by a teacher.

Unrelated ideas? Not at all! *Through each of these discussions runs the theme of rejection.* First, Bob was rejected by his *parents* in their divorce. Then he experienced rejection from the *coach.* His *girl* also had begun to show a lack of interest. And when the *teacher* criticized his work, Bob once again felt he wasn't being accepted. This type of theme is important in every counseling experience. The successful counselor is alert to all of these relationships and is quick to spot the tie between seemingly unrelated events.

Limit Each Interview

It is generally wise to spend no more than one hour for one counseling session. The reason for this is that a longer period usually produces too much material to be worked on effectively. The same principle is applicable to the number of topics to be considered in one session. During the first few interviews you may consider in a general way a wide range of topics such as friends, school, parents and spiritual matters. After this, however, it is usually best to focus on only one or two major ideas in each interview. This encourages more thorough treatment of each area and makes the material more significant and easier to remember. If in one session a counselee discusses his attitude toward his father, his feelings of depression, his vocational aspirations and his dating life, he will likely have trouble remembering the most significant thoughts. Of course, it may turn out that all of these areas are related to a basic problem of feelings of inadequacy and thus belong together. In most cases, however, it is best to center on one or two central issues during each session.

Help the Counselee to Understand Himself

This concept is considered under several other headings, but it is so simple and basic that it is sometimes overlooked in the maze of more complex techniques. Everything you do in the counseling session should be directed toward this end. Help the counselee to understand himself. The following is a question which can be phrased many times during counseling: "Now that we have discussed this considerably, do you think you understand why you have been feeling and acting the way you have?" If the counselee can answer this question in the affirmative, you have gone a long way toward a resolution of the maladjustment.

Never Argue

Some counselors are ineffective because they become involved in arguments with their counselees. This is a serious error and should be avoided. It is not your responsibility to win every person over to your side. It is your responsibility to help the counselee see all aspects of a problem and carefully trace the causes and then find solutions. You can express your personal feeling and turn to the Word for guidance, but beyond this the decision is in the counselee's hand. He is responsible to the Lord for his decisions. When a counselor finds himself arguing with a counselee, it is usually because the counselor himself feels insecure and easily threatened. By winning someone over to his view, the counselor thinks he increases his own feelings of success and worthiness. This personal involvement can be a serious hindrance to successful counseling.

Take a Long Range View

One of the most common signs of emotional immaturity is an emphasis on the present with a lack of ability to plan for the future. Almost every person suffering from emotional problems is tied up in the urgency of immediate actions. Their thoughts are in the present. They are unable to gain a long range viewpoint. As a counselor it is your privilege to uphold this mature planning in the face of the counselee's weakness. Of course it does little good to tell a person to "take a long range view." This is a process that only comes with added emotional maturity. Yet you must be alert lest you be caught up in a sense of urgency for the immediate at the expense of the long range perspective. A counselee, for example, may be confused by a current dating crisis. It's up to you to work through the entire situation and help him come to see the ultimate worth of this situation in terms of added maturity, increased experience and greater spiritual understanding. This is one of the greatest challenges in counseling young people and it is one that comes slowly.

Obtain the Divine Perspective

Closely related to a long range viewpoint is obtaining a Biblical perspective of the person and his problem. Difficulties often center upon a misunderstanding of trials and temptations. When passing through a trying circumstance, it is hard to see the value and worth of the experience. Only after it is passed, and we look back, can the full impact of the trials be viewed. During the difficulty, however, a person can experience the calm assurance that if he is following the guidance of the Holy Spirit, this trial is ordained of God for a planned purpose in greater growth. The Book of James is especially helpful in this matter — dealing with the difference between trials and temptations and with the importance of developing patience as a result of trials. You do your counselee a great service as you lead him to an understanding and acceptance of many seemingly unreconcilable and distressing events.

Distinguish Between the Causes and the Symptoms

Unless you understand the causes — how they develop, how they produce certain behavior — you cannot expect to bring more than limited help to a person. The unwanted behavior — constant headaches, or extreme bashfulness, or compulsive stealing, etc., is the result — the blossom. But this behavior is not the cause. The causes, like root systems, are often hidden.

When you counsel, focus your attention not only on the apparent problem, but also on the "not so apparent" roots. If you merely cut off a blossom from a bush, you have really not eliminated the bush. The root system is still there, and in a short time more blossoms will develop.

Many counselors have made the mistake of focusing on the symptoms (the behavior) rather than the causes. For example, a camp counselor was asked by a camper about the problem of speaking in public. "I simply can't talk in public. I freeze up, and stand there like a mummy," said the boy. The counselor, not thinking about the causes began to focus on the symptom — then proceeded to tell the camper that he had to overcome the problem: "You've just got to pull yourself together, and get up there and make yourself known." The counselor continued to give free advice, concentrating on the behavior rather than the causes. Naturally, he didn't provide much help. In fact, the boy felt worse. How different it would have been if the counselor had encouraged the camper to first express himself, then look at the causes.

Trace the Origins

Several points already discussed are particularly important in tracing the origins of an emotional or spiritual problem. One of these is to encourage complete discussion. As a problem is talked through, many insights into the sources of difficulty will be discovered. A second basic technique is to listen carefully for any major themes in the counselee's verbalizations. Another important means of finding the real difficulty is to continually ask yourself and the counselee, "Why did that happen?" or "What caused you to feel that way?"

You should try to find the first instances of any maladaptive feeling which is bothering your counselee. Janet, for example, had a fear of entering into any group situation. Her counselor asked if she had ever felt this way during high school. "Oh, yes, many times," replied Janet. Then she went on to relate several such instances of apprehension. The counselor then asked her to tell about her experiences in elementary school.

She did this and recalled that even in the lower grades she was afraid to speak in front of the class or to answer any question the teacher raised. As Janet and the counselor gradually moved back to her early experiences, they found that as a very young girl she had been criticized and rebuked by her father. He offered her no love or acceptance, and she had become afraid to express herself to him. These initial experiences had established a pattern of insecurity which had hindered her adjustment throughout her school years. But once she had found the source of the problem Janet began to make rapid progress in overcoming these attitudes.

Another important technique in tracing the causes of problem behavior is to carefully discuss the counselee's relationship to his parents and other significant figures. *Most serious problems are closely tied to the person's early experiences with his family.* You can raise questions such as, "Tell me about your father. What type of man was he?" "What kind of discipline did you receive as a child?" "Did your parents frequently criticize you, or were they generous with praise and compliments?" "Who was the more aggressive person in your home?" and "Did your parents have a happy marriage?" A discussion of these and similar areas often brings to light some of the major sources of problems. This is one of the best ways to uncover the deeper roots of emotional disturbances.

Avoid Hasty Conclusions

If the previous steps of discussion and tracing the origins of problems are followed, there will be no problem in making hasty decisions. Just a word of warning though: rapid decisions are generally based on impulsive thinking and a lack of real insight into the problem. This is to be avoided in the counseling process. Sound conclusions are rarely forced; they emerge.

Lead the Counselee to a Deeper Knowledge of Christ

The greatest contribution you can make in life is to lead a person to a saving knowledge of Christ, and to help him walk closer to the Lord. This is the ultimate aim of counseling. It is not enough merely to turn out emotionally rather well-adjusted individuals. The Christian counselor should have as his primary goal the counselee's effective relationship with Jesus Christ. There may be many emotional problems that need to be solved, some of them hindering spiritual growth. But the ultimate objective is to deepen the counselee's daily spiritual life. As you lead him into a better understanding of the Word of God and the importance of complete yieldedness to the Holy Spirit, the counselee begins to move into paths of Christian maturity and service. In addition, the Lord will give him the insight and support to handle many spiritual and emotional conflicts which will arise in the future.

Challenge Your Counselee

Closely related to a deepened spiritual life is the matter of challenging your counselee. This important consideration pervades many aspects of life. First of all, the young person needs to be challenged to completely dedicate his life to the Lord and to gain a real burden for service and soul winning. He can also be challenged to obtain a quality Christian education which will prepare him most effectively for the Lord's use. A basic characteristic of youth is the desire to accept a challenge. You have the wonderful opportunity to capitalize on this youthful energy and optimism. Many of the world's most dynamic Christian witnesses have been men and women who accepted the challenge to go all out for God when still in their teens.

Help the Counselee Build a Close Relationship to His Parents

One of the problems common to nearly every teen-ager is some degree of strained relationship with his parents. This may take the form of rebellion and utter disregard for parental authority, or it may be a much more subtle factor of feeling misunderstood by the "older generation." The emotional stability and growth provided by a well-adjusted home is much more effective in working behavior changes than any therapeutic effort.

You can help your counselee to gain a better understanding of why his parents feel as they do. Then he can discover some of the sources of misunderstanding. Teen-agers need to communicate with their parents, and most adults do desire this relationship. When you help break down family discord and restore broken communication lines, you are building within your counselee one of the strongest barriers against further maladjustments.

Some counselors try deliberately to set a young person against his parents. These unwise counselors feel that they can get closer to the teen-ager if they hop on the bandwagon and criticize and ridicule the parents. But young people do not appreciate this. Even though they may outwardly enjoy having someone to side with them against their parents, nearly all teen-agers have a measure of respect and pride in their parents and do not want others to criticize and condemn them. *Young people come to you to re-establish broken relationships, not to tear down already sagging ones.* Care must be taken to identify closely with the counselee, but at the same time not to put him at odds with his parents. When you reach this balance, you greatly increase the significance and duration of your counseling ministry.

Summarize the Session

An important technique of interviewing is to use the last few minutes of a session to summarize and evaluate the material just discussed. During the emotional involvement of the counseling hour, the counselee may find it difficult to remember key concepts and feelings. By taking a few minutes at the close of each session to recap the discussion, you firmly place these primary thoughts into perspective. You may even suggest that the counselee write down three or four of the most important concepts. A portion of this summary might go as follows: "Mark, we have a few minutes left. Let's make use of them to summarize several points. We have discussed some of the reasons that seem to cause you to lose your temper so easily. Let's jot these ideas down so we can go into them further next time. First, you told me that you used to really get angry with your dad. That seems to be one of the most important factors, doesn't it? You got in the pattern of fighting back at an early age. Then we saw that when you don't get your own way you often resent other people. You feel that they are trying to prevent you from getting something you want. This seems to be important too. You also said that part of this was probably a spiritual problem.

If you were closer to the Lord you would let Him control your feelings more. These three ideas are very important. Why don't you do some thinking about them during the week and we can discuss them again next time?"

Such a summary helps the counselee to view the most important aspects of the counseling hour. Without this, many sessions seem to have been very interesting and profitable, but the main concepts are forgotten. And *you* do not always need to do the summarizing. You can ask the counselee to give the several points he felt were most important. If he restates them, the summary is even more significant.

Responsibility for Referrals

One of the significant marks of a mature counselor is the recognition of one's own limitations. Counselers have specialties. Some are particularly trained in dealing with emotional problems. Others are well-qualified for counseling with minor emotional difficulties and important spiritual problems. Medical personnel are trained to care for the physical aspect of maladjustments. When you counsel you can evaluate the problem and see where the person can get the most effective assistance. If you are qualified to help him, fine! If not, recognize your limitations, and help him locate a person who is especially qualified to deal with his particular problem.

You will want to be acquainted with the types of services available by different specialists. If the problem is obviously a spiritual problem, and you feel it is beyond you, suggest that the counselee speak with a minister who knows and loves the Word. If the problem is vocational or occupational, suggest a school counselor or a person specializing in tests of ability, aptitude and vocation selection. When the problem appears to be a physical one, refer to a local physician. If the difficulty is obviously a severe personality disturbance of a long standing nature, refer to a Christian psychologist or psychiatrist. By utilizing these available referrals, you can help the counselee to secure the finest assistance possible.

QUESTIONS FOR DISCUSSION

1. How can a counselor develop proper rapport with a counselee?

2. List several goals in short-term counseling.

3. What may prevent a counselee from revealing his basic problem during a first or second session?

4. Why do many people with problems expect "quick answers"?

5. What is meant by "ventilating a problem"?

6. How does a person gain insight into his problem?

7. How can a counselor help a counselee to develop independence and self-direction?

8. What is the significance of the old saying, "Friends listen, but enemies talk"?

9. What is meant by the statement, "Counseling is a process, not a lecture"?

10. How does full discussion benefit a counselee?

11. How can a counselor demonstrate God's unconditional acceptance?

12. Explain the statement, "Sin is a reality and must be dealt with in a real way."

13. Why should a counselor not express shock at anything a counselee says?

14. What is the value of open-end questions in counseling?

15. How and why might a counselor avoid answering questions which a counselee asks?

16. Give an example of *reflecting* a statement or question expressed by a counselee.

17. How does a counselor help a counselee to clarify his feelings?

18. What is meant by "themes" in data which a counselee brings to light?

19. Why is it important to limit the amount of time for a counseling session?

20. What may cause a counselor to argue with his counselee?

21. Why should a counselor focus on the causes, rather than the symptoms of a problem?

22. How can a counselee be led to a deeper knowledge of Christ?

23. What is the significance of the statement, "A basic characteristic of youth is the desire to accept a challenge"?

24. How can a counselor help a counselee to build a closer relationship with his parents?

25. Discuss the techniques of summarizing a counseling session.

6

Problems of Children and Youth

As you counsel with children and youth, you will be confronted with many types of problems. Some will be minor, but others will be extremely serious. These will cover a wide range of physical, emotional, social and spiritual maladjustments.

In this chapter we will consider some of the most frequent types of problems which children and young people have. As you counsel, you will want to keep several factors in mind: (1) Is this behavior unusual, or is it normal for his or her age level? (2) Does this problem involve other young people in this particular setting? If so, what action should be taken? (3) Are there established policies and procedures which I should follow? (4) Should there be communication with parents, and if so who is responsible for this? Youth counselors seldom function independently. They work in cooperation with staff members, and are responsible to others. Counselors, therefore, should consider their service to a counselee, and at the same time not overlook their limitations and their responsibility for referrals.

The Counselor's Precedures and Resources

As you counsel with young people, you can utilize the following resources. They will help you to be more effective and cause your counseling to have lasting results.

Scripture: Use Scripture freely. Since it is God's Word it will not return void, but it will help to establish great eternal truths in one's life.

Books: There are many books to which you can refer. Your discussion with a young person may be limited, but you can usually refer him to books at a Christian bookstore. Appropriate Christian literature can influence him for weeks or months while he is perhaps unable to see a counselor.

Church: You may be limited in your contacts with a person, but you can encourage him to attend a Bible-believing church where he can receive further encouragement, teaching and fellowship.

Christian schools: Many problems of youth stem from the fact that they are not receiving Christian instruction and not having Christian friendships. A young person can be helped greatly by being encouraged to attend a Christian school.

Additional referrals: If a boy or girl has a severe problem, do not hesitate to refer him to others for additional help. Your short-term counseling may uncover problems, but it may not bring assistance which is needed. In this event you will be wise to refer young people to other church or camp staff members, to various agencies or to recognized specialists.

Aggression and Hostility

Perhaps the most socially upsetting of all emotional problems is the angry, rebellious individual. In a church activity this person is likely to be argumentative and uncooperative. At camp he may disobey his leaders, disrupt activities and actually engage in physical fighting. Unlike the quiet, withdrawn person, this aggressive, hostile person cannot be tolerated. His influence can hinder the effectiveness of the best-planned program. Unless the behavior is suppressed or altered, many of the group can miss the blessings of a class or camp experience.

The hostile person generally feels insecure and unwanted. When he does not get his way, he fights back at that person or object which has frustrated his goal. Unconsciously he may direct his hostility toward innocent adults or young people. When someone attacks his self-esteem, the hostile person reacts with anger in an attempt to protect his poor self-concept. One frequent cause of anger and rebellion is *parental rejection*. When a child is deprived of his natural need for love and affection, he frequently becomes angry. He has been deprived of one of the most important things in life. Since he thinks he got a "raw deal," he feels justified in fighting back at society.

A *broken home* is frequently at the base of strong feelings of anger and rebellion. Like the rejected child, the person coming from a home torn by divorce or death has missed out on many of man's basic emotional needs. He has not had the opportunity to learn to love, since no one has shown him affection. The alternative to love is hate. If a child does not learn to love, it is natural for him to develop the opposite emotion: anger.

Some rebellious young people are reacting to *poor discipline*. Studies of delinquents show that the families of these teen-agers are frequently markedly deficient in discipline. In some cases there was unduly strict and harsh punishment. In others the parents were grossly inconsistent. The child did not know what to expect from one moment to the next. In still other cases there was an almost total absence of guidance. The child was left on his own to do as he pleased. Without proper discipline or guidance, he learned to seek only his own gratification. He developed no feeling for the rights and privileges of others.

As he grows older he resents any attempt to place restrictions on his behavior, since he is concerned only with himself. Society is a structure to be fought, not a group to be a member of. Authority is to be resented, not respected. Other people are to be used as objects, not enjoyed or appreciated as human beings.

Some children who appear to be ornery and mean are actually very seriously disturbed. As a counselor you should be alert to symptoms of *severe emotional disturbances*. When a person is extremely rebellious and angry, he may be a seriously maladjusted individual in need of concentrated professional attention.

A *lack of spiritual conversion and growth* is a basic factor in feelings of anger and hostility. Man is by nature a sinful, self-centered being. Outside of Christ it is only natural to seek to satisfy one's own wants and to neglect the rights of others. When a person is attacked, the natural thing is to rebel or defend oneself. But once a person has experienced a personal relationship with Jesus Christ, he has a new resource for overcoming the natural tendency of the old sin nature. Anger and resentment can be replaced with love and acceptance. Rebellion can be replaced with cooperation.

In counseling with a rebellious person, both the individual and the group must be taken into account. If you are in a church or camp setting where the group is being disturbed, *you may have to be very firm with definite discipline.* If a complete service or activity is being disrupted, it is no time to sweetly plead with an angry teen-ager to "please cooperate." The good of the individual may have to be temporarily suspended for the benefit of many. Definite restrictions and discipline may be required to replace chaos with order.

Even when a firm hand of discipline must be applied, *you can do this in an accepting manner.* Children do not think less of you when you correct their obvious misbehavior. On the contrary, they generally respect you more highly. It is when they continually manipulate and coerce others that rebellious youth lose their respect for authority.

When you are able to counsel a rebellious young person, one of the first things to do is to *allow him to ventilate his strong feelings of hostility.* He needs the opportunity to express his true feelings of hate and anger before he is free to search for their causes.

As a counselee gives vent to his feelings, you can *raise questions about the source of his feelings.* Attitudes toward parents are especially important in many cases of hostility. When the young person finds the causes of his problem, he can see that his actions are actually an attempt to protect himself and to seek his own way. When this insight comes, he is ready for an application of the truth of the Scriptures.

A personal relationship to Christ places God at the center of one's life. It is no longer self which must be defended and protected. Jesus Christ is the Master of life and He does not need to be defended in anger. A growing spiritual relationship under the guidance of the Holy Spirit enables the believer to overcome feelings of anger and resentment. The love of God begins to penetrate into the previous unloved heart. The quiet acceptance and care of the Lord begins to replace the instability and rejection of an earthly parent. The motivation of serving self is shoved aside to allow for a new principle of love. These and other spiritual concepts can sink deeply into the heart of every believer whose life is controlled by the Lord. "But the fruit of the Spirit is love, joy, peace, longsuffering, gentleness, goodness, faith, meekness, temperance: against such there is no law" (Galatians 5:22, 23).

ATTENTION GETTING

Every church, school and camp has at least one (usually several) attention-getters. This person may be a "clown" or a very annoying individual. The "clown" is most easy to accept, and may even be an asset to the group. He may, however, have similar emotional needs as the person with upsetting and annoying actions. They too have chosen different means of seeking the attention they need.

Continuously calling attention to oneself by devious actions often results from *a lack of attention and affection at home*. When a child is rejected and unloved, he craves the interest of others. If he cannot get this attention through pleasant and appropriate behavior, he will develop other means. An important concept to recognize is the fact that an extremely obedient child who strives to please at every turn, and the obnoxious attention-getter may be striving to fill the same needs. The quieter child searches for love by pleasing and making himself useful and needed. The more active child seeks the same attention and affection through his overt misbehavior.

Overindulgent or insecure parents may instill in their children a pattern of reaction which centers upon attention getting. By continually putting a young child on display to the friends and neighbors and having him "show off," the parents are teaching the child to obtain attention by being the star attraction. As the child leaves home, he has learned his lesson well. At church or at school he knows he can gain attention by showing off, joking or by disrupting the activity at hand.

When faced with a child or youth who is disrupting school or camp activities, it is important to realize the causes for his actions. This person is seeking attention and affection. If he were getting enough love and interest from those in his environment, he would not have to turn to misbehavior or clowning. Consequently, one of the first things to do with this person is to *give him attention for desirable behavior*. When he is praised and complimented for appropriate actions, the need to show off will be lessened. At the same time, the *disruptive behavior should be ignored as much as possible*. If the attention-getting devices fail, he will search for other avenues of acceptance. As you ignore the maladaptive behavior, and praise

and encourage appropriate actions, the person can learn a
more effective means of adapting to his environment in his
search for attention. In most settings you can utilize the child's
emotional need by giving him special jobs. He may be asked
to deliver a daily attendance report, or to help arrange the
classroom or cabin. He can be called upon to read Scripture
verses or answer questions. This gives him attention for desirable actions and lessens the need for undesirable behavior.

When older youth become an obvious behavioral problem,
you may be wise to *speak confidentially to them about their
actions*. This takes much tact and you must establish a good
relationship in order for your suggestions to be accepted. If
one of these young people does recognize he has a problem,
you can then arrange several sessions to discuss the matter
more fully. During these sessions you will want to search for
the causes of the behavior. You should also discuss the effect
of his actions on others. The very behavior that is meant to
gain attention may actually alienate a young person from the
group. When he sees that he is defeating his own goals, he
may turn to more adaptive behavior. As a person comes to
understand the unmet emotional needs which are causing the
inappropriate actions, these needs begin to lose their hold.
They can be replaced by the joy of knowing that God is
interested in him and accepts him. With the development of
a closer walk with the Lord, the young person finds his day
filled with things which glorify God. He has less time and less
need to seek the attention of others, since he is more concerned
with the wonderful plan which God has for his life.

BEDWETTING

In nearly every group of children and youth the problem of
bedwetting (enuresis) arises. Most authorities agree that continuous bedwetting beyond the age of approximately four
years is probably evidence of emotional stress and strain rather
than of a mere transitory problem.

Among the more common causes of bedwetting is *a tense
home setting*. The child who lives in an atmosphere of anxiety
and tension is more likely to develop many emotional conflicts
and symptoms. Enuresis is sometimes an outgrowth of an en-

vironment of parental instability, bickering, criticism or rejection.

Related to a poor home environment is the *need for attention*. One sure way to obtain the attention of others is by wetting the bed. Although this attention may be negative and even result in punishment, the rejected child would rather have this negative attention than none at all.

Some parents place *undue emphasis on bladder control at an early age*. By trying to force a child to control his urinations before he is capable, the parents create many feelings of conflict and frustration within the child. Later, when he does have the physiological development to maintain voluntary control, the anxiety and conflict associated with early attempts at bladder control interfere with the normal process of development. Parents should not be too harsh on children who wet the bed, since some research studies indicate that bedwetters often have parents who had the same difficulty when they were young.

A *new and threatening environment* may cause some children to temporarily lose bladder control. When a child is somewhat fearful and insecure, a new situation may emphasize his nervousness and anxiety and result in bedwetting. With a return to a more secure and stable home environment, this temporary difficulty disappears.

In a camp setting with young children, you can usually do little to overcome the basic problem in bedwetting. You can, however, utilize a number of practical considerations. When you find a child who wets his bed, you can *equip him with a rubber sheet. Care should be taken not to mention this problem to other campers* since this will only embarrass and make the situation worse. *By limiting the child's liquid consumption* in the evening, you lessen the likelihood of serious bedwetting. You will also want to *be sure that he goes to the bathroom just before bedtime* and *possibly awaken him once during the* night for the same purpose.

If you are counseling with an older child, an adolescent or young adult, who is still bothered by bedwetting, you should *evaluate his total personality adjustment*. Little help can generally be obtained by merely discussing possible sources of the bedwetting. Instead, the young person should discuss his total adjustment, his self-concept, his feelings of insecurity, lack of confidence or rejection. As these larger issues are evaluated and overcome, the problem of bedwetting will generally disappear, even though it is not directly discussed during the interviews. The reason for this is that bedwetting is often a symptom of an underlying problem. It is a sign saying there is something wrong emotionally. Only as the underlying psychological conflicts are dispelled, will the symptom of bedwetting disappear.

DATING

Problems of dating are frequently expressed by young people. This is only natural. The physical, intellectual, social and emotional development of a young person has reached the point where they are interested in the opposite sex. However, this attraction is much more than a sexual interest. Boys and girls in the adolescent and young adult years are exploring their self-concepts. They are wanting to be considered as worthwhile and interesting. They are also desiring to learn more about others — wanting to give as well as receive affection.

All of these basic drives culminate in a desire to develop special friendships — to have dates. When counseling with young people about dating problems, remember that there are a number of psychological factors (conscious or unconscious) involved. This basic concept will help you to be a more thoughtful, effective counselor.

Dating Age

Young people often ask, either in a group or individually, about the proper age to begin dating. This question comes more frequently from girls than from boys, because girls are generally more mature than boys of the same age, and girls feel that they must wait until they are asked for a date.

Questions about the proper age for dating often come from young teen-agers. But the same question is often in the minds of older teen-agers. There is a great difference in the general maturity of young people. For example, a girl of 15 may be more mature than a girl of 16. Too, they may come from homes with a variety of standards and beliefs about dating. Some parents have a general understanding and rule that dating is not to begin until a certain age. In another family the parents themselves dated early, and, in fact, were married as teen-agers. So they may feel that early dating is in order.

In counseling with young people about proper dating age, you can keep several things in mind:

Encourage full discussion. Merely giving the young person an opportunity to express his feelings and talk about the problem will benefit him. In some instances very little more needs to be done.

Help him to understand the true causes of his feelings. For example, a girl may complain that her parents will not let her date or that she has to get in from her dates at an "unreasonably early" hour. But as you talk with her, you may discover that her problem is really not dating. Rather, her problem may be that she is unsuccessful and unhappy at school. Her concern about dating is actually an attempt to run away from unpleasant school experiences. As you counsel with young people, keep in mind the various possibilities that might prompt their concern about dating.

Encourage young people to consider their parents' attitudes regarding early dating. Help them put themselves in the place of their mothers and fathers and see what considerations they come up with. One of the best ways to encourage young people to think through their parents' attitude is to use a short reaction story such as this: "Janet thinks that she is mature enough to go on dates, but her parents feel that she is not. Why do her parents feel as they do?" Such a counseling technique, especially with groups, makes it easy for young people to assume the role of their mothers and dads, thereby causing teen-agers to think the problem through more thoroughly.

Crushes

There are many kinds of crushes. Boy-girl, adolescent-adult, and others. A teen-ager may have a crush on a camp counselor, a teacher, a speaker, or anyone whom he admires and imagines he could love.

Why do such crushes develop? Because of the instability of a teen-ager, because they may have been starved for love and affection at home, or because they have not yet established satisfying relationships generally with other young people. They are often loners.

How can a counselor handle these problems? (1) Let the counselee talk it out. (2) Help him to see what is causing this behavior. (3) Encourage him to become more realistic. Help him to see that a camp director, for instance (if such a person is the object of his crush), is friendly to all the campers and not especially enamored by one. (4) Lead the counselee into a closer walk with the Lord Jesus Christ. Point out the fact that God loves and cares for him and wants to meet his needs.

Dating the Unsaved

Many young people are either dating an unsaved person or considering doing so. They may try to justify themselves by saying, "I want to lead him to Christ," or "I want to get him into the church."

What are the true causes behind a Christian young person wanting to date someone who is unsaved? A person may not see the seriousness of the situation. He may not be "Bible-taught."

Some are lonely. Clara, for example, lives in a small community where there are no Christian boys her age. She feels that it is better to date an unsaved boy than not to date at all.

Some young people with deep feelings of insecurity will date anyone. It tends to bolster their egos — making them feel wanted. The person who dates almost anyone, saved or not, may not be saved himself.

Christians who date the unsaved may not be dedicated. They may be following Christ afar off — disobedient and rebellious.

Problems of dating the unsaved can be resolved as the counselor uncovers the true causes, then leads the counselee to meet his basic needs in ways that honor Christ. Counselors often help young people avoid tragedies by encouraging them to let Christ have His way in their lives — including dating.

Having No Dates

When a young person or an adult has the problem of not

dating, help him to understand the true nature of his problem. In most instances there are factors which, if understood and resolved, can enable a person to date as much as he desires.

It may be a personality problem. It can also stem from an unusual fear of the opposite sex because of experiences in childhood. Whatever the case, encourage several sessions of counseling.

Sometimes you can make practical suggestions. For example, Helen tries too hard. She is overly aggressive and frightens the boys away. Bill, on the other hand, is too crude. He has few manners. If he could learn to be polite and improve his conversation skills, girls would like him better.

Gus doesn't have dates because his appearance is sagging. His features are good enough, but his hair is never combed, he is not shaved, his hair is never trimmed and he even has a personal problem of body odor. Little wonder he is not the first choice among girls!

Sue, on the other hand, isn't having many dates with Christian fellows because she is spiritually immature. The boys who are dedicated Christians don't want to waste their time with her.

Connie has virtually no dates because she is extremely shy. Her problem is long-standing, requiring much counseling and possibly professional help.

As a counselor you can help young people understand their specific problems. People can change, and you can be used of God to bring about a marked improvement in others.

Petting

Young people hold different ideas about petting. These concepts are a reflection of their own thinking as well as the standards of their homes. You can help a young person avoid serious tragedies by sitting quietly with him or his group and discussing the implications of petting. Group discussion is effective inasmuch as well-adjusted young people with wholesome attitudes will usually express themselves freely and influence others their own age. Discussions should not only take the form of warnings (although they are important); they should also include solid reasons and an appeal to the dedicated life in Christ.

It is helpful to a young person to come to an understanding

of why he wants to engage in petting. He may feel, for example, that he will be considered "different" or "inadequate" if he doesn't. His petting activities may stem from a lack of sex education. So it goes! There are many reasons why a person may be engaging in petting, and he should be led to an understanding of his actions.

Petting leads to more serious petting, and more serious petting leads to sexual involvement. This often brings about intimate relationships. And intimate relationships often result in the birth of another human being. The counselor should point out that petting is definitely a part of love-making in marriage. When taken out of its rightful setting and brought into dating, it can — and often does — produce disastrous consequences.

The greatest deterrent to loose living is devotion to Jesus Christ. When the Lord begins to reign in a person's life, he is convicted of his wrongdoing. And with this conviction and surrender comes the sustaining power of God.

Going Steady

There are many reasons why young people want to go steady. Some are valid, and others not. A girl, for example, may want to go steady because she does not have a dependable date. She wants to be sure she has a partner for social activities — that she isn't going to miss out on anything because of a lack of a date.

A boy may want to go steady because he feels he can take more liberties than if he dated many girls. Still another person may want to go steady because he thinks it is the proper thing to do. A girl may feel like a back number if she can't tell her friends about her going steady. Naturally, your job as a counselor is to help her see that as a child of God she is not responsible to the crowd, but she *is* responsible to the Lord. She can't help what *others* do, but she *can* control what *she* does. As you counsel with young people about going steady, help them to understand that one of the main purposes of dating is to get to know many different young people.

As you encourage discussion and enable young people to learn the true motives of their actions, they will become more mature and thoughtful. As they are led into a close relationship with Christ, they will want to obey and please Him in all that they do.

DRESS AND GROOMING

During the teen years most young people go through a clothing fad. This is common and is to be expected by the young person seeking status among the group and trying to exert his independence from parental control. Some, however, dress in an obviously inappropriate manner. Boys may wear "jeans" or "cut offs" to a meeting where only neat sport clothes are appropriate. Girls, too, may wear bold and inappropriate clothes as well as provocative dress.

One of the basic causes for this lack of conventionality is a *need for attention.* The person who feels insecure and rejected may try to gain the attention of others by conspicuous attire.

Feelings of anger and rebelliousness are often associated with improper dress. The teen-ager who is generally disgusted with parental authority may seek to assert his independence and rebellious spirit by refusing to adjust to society's customs.

Girls who dress provocatively, or appear as scantily clad as possible at the pool or beach, frequently have *strong feelings of inadequacy in their feminine sexual role.* By exhibiting as much of the body as possible, the girl who needs to be re-assured of her sexual adequacy can gain the attentive look of others.

The lack of parental guidance is another common factor in inadequate dress. When a girl's mother takes no interest or concern in her daughter's dress, the girl can be easily swayed by the pull of the world to cheap and improper attire.

The desire to be an accepted member of the peer group causes some girls to fall in line with very liberal trends of dress and conduct. In the attempt to be accepted, a girl may compromise her standards and ignore the guidance of her parents.

A *lack of spiritual dedication* is a very important factor in inappropriate and provocative dress. When a Christian girl is living a carnal life, she is not concerned about upholding strong Christian ideals and conduct. She is susceptible to many unwholesome influences.

Most Christian young people will respond to suggestions

regarding dress if they are presented in an appropriate manner. Rather than scolding a teen-ager for his dress, you can raise the point more subtly by *asking him a question about his attire.* If you are close to the young person, you can be free to *frankly discuss the importance of appropriate dress,* both for one's own personal satisfaction and for the impression he makes on others.

The influence of group pressure and the desire for attention should be carefully evaluated with the person. With some teen-agers the problem of dress should be considered in terms of *a broader problem of dedication to spiritual standards.* The provocative dress may only be one manifestation of a life which is not fully committed to Christ. In your counseling you can *help this person to see the need for a relationship to the Lord which permeates his entire life.* When the matter of a closer walk with the Lord is settled, the Holy Spirit will convict a person of inappropriate dress. You will not have to continually correct, but can watch the Lord work miracles in every area of the person's adjustment.

Educational and Vocational Planning

Youth counselors have a special responsibility to help young people utilize their God-given talents. Nearly everyone wants to be successful. But Christians have the added opportunity of living a life of spiritual significance and lasting value.

The most important step in making the correct vocational and educational choices is *total surrender to the Lord.* When the Holy Spirit is controlling the life of the believer, all other decisions fall into place. Without the guidance of the Lord, no one can expect to make proper judgments. "Adequate" decisions may be made, but the best answers which the Lord has will never be obtained without His guidance. The Scriptures say, "I will instruct thee and teach thee in the way which thou shalt go: I will guide thee with mine eye" (Psalm 32:8).

An important concept given in James 1:17 is that *"Every good gift and every perfect gift is from above."* Every talent of personality, intelligence or other ability is a gift of God. And it is the privilege and duty of the Christian to use these in the service of the Lord. Once a person has surrendered his life to Christ, and realizes that his abilities are God-given, he is on the road to successful vocational adjustment.

Once these decisions are made, the Lord expects the believer to utilize all possible means to find the work to which he is called. God does not mysteriously hide His will for lives behind a veil of secrecy. Instead He gradually unfolds His guidance through daily experiences and evaluations.

Educational Choices

A basic choice for all young people is the selection of a college. It is here that many of life's decisions are made. Permanent friendships are developed and a life's partner may be found. The final vocational choice is often made as well as decisions influencing emotional and spiritual growth. The choice of a college should be made with earnest prayer and consideration. One of the greatest influences in the life of a young person can come through the experiences gained at a Christian college.

There was a time when an institution that advertised itself as a Christian college was truly one. But that is not always true today. A genuinely Christian institution is one in which the president and every member of the faculty is a born-again believer, and where the Bible is upheld as the inspired Word of God. In such a college, there is constant, special emphasis on soul-winning. Although a Christian college is not designed as a cure-all for the problems of all young people, it can have a tremendous influence in molding the lives of young people into mature and stable Christians.

One of the advantages of a Christian college or Bible school is the personal interest shown each student. There is nothing quite so wonderful and stimulating as knowing that those around you are interested in you, desiring that you do well. This is characteristic of a Christian school. Non-Christian institutions are not void of this quality, but teachers who do not know Christ cannot possibly have the same devotion to their students as those who do know Him.

The quality of scholarship of a fine Christian college is usually better than that of a non-Christian institution. Christian teachers have access to secular knowledge, and in addition, they have spiritual understanding that non-Christians do not possess.

Of special importance are the *friendships* one develops at Christian colleges and Bible schools. As a person grows older, he appreciates the fact that he utilizes and profits from his Christian contacts. The evangelical Christian school has friendships which one will cherish throughout life.

One of the important activities of college-age people is *dating*. College students should have the opportunity to meet many other Christians their own age from whom they can choose a life partner. It is not unusual to find the "pickings" very slim in a non-Christian college where there may be only a handful of Christians. *It is not enough for a Christian to marry another Christian.* One should have the opportunity to date many fine Christians in the process of finding God's choice of a mate.

At a Christian college *one learns and practices Christian conduct.* It is often on such campuses that young people learn the joy of total dedication to Christ. It is there that they rise above worldly standards and reach a place of Christian experience where God can use them mightily. Some Christian young people know very little about proper Christian conduct. They may not know the joy of living out-and-out for Christ, and experiencing the blessings that accompany true consecration.

A distinct advantage of a Christian college is the *daily study of God's Word*. Outstanding Bible teachers are on the staff to teach required Bible courses. The nation's outstanding laymen and ministers speak at daily chapel services. The ideal time to learn the Word of God thoroughly is in one's youth. If a person doesn't build thorough Bible knowledge into his life in his teens and early twenties, he'll probably never do it. And to neglect such training is to disregard the most important preparation in life.

A Christian college is a wonderful place to *learn God's will*. There is no place where a young person can learn of the opportunities for Christian service as well as he can in a Christian school. It is there that needs of various mission fields are carefully presented. Student groups are organized to learn more about the opportunities of Christian service. Leaders of

different Christian organizations come to the campus for interviews. This exposure to many opportunities for Christian service
has repeatedly been the source of God's leading one into His
service.

One sometimes hears the statement that a person has more
opportunities for *witnessing* on a non-Christian campus. This
is seldom the case. Nearly every evangelical Christian school
has a program whereby all students learn to witness in jails,
distribute tracts, give testimonies at various services, make
house-to-house visits and take part in many other activities.
Actually most students attending Christian colleges engage in
witnessing much more than those attending non-Christian institutions. And such activities in a Christian school are consistent
and well-planned.

Going away to a Christian college usually means *getting
away from home, parents and old friends*. This is usually a
distinct advantage. Unfortunately many Christian young people
never leave their parents until they get married. As wonderful
as it is to have the influence of godly parents, it is also ad-
vantageous to get in a new environment where one cannot
turn to Mother or Dad for every decision. This helps young
people become self-reliant and independent. It develops self-
confidence and poise.

These and other factors make the advantage of attending a
Christian school significant. One of your opportunities as a
counselor of youth is to help guide them into an understanding
of some of these values in selecting a college. You can render
a great service by having catalogs from a number of fine
schools available for the use of your young people. A "Christian
college night," or similar emphasis, may also be effective in
giving direction to youth.

Of course, one need not attend a Christian school to learn
surrender and dedication. But in an evangelical institution
where one receives such training, it is natural to develop into
a consecrated Christian whom God can use in a special way.

Vocational Selection

As you counsel with young people about their life's vocation,
the following points can be of significance if evaluated carefully:

1. Consider your intellectual abilities.

2. What are your aptitudes and special abilities?
3. What have your high school grades been?
4. Weigh your character and personality traits.
5. Do you have any physical handicaps?
6. What are your main interests?
7. Talk with men and women in various professions.
8. Read literature on different occupations.
9. Take part-time jobs in a vocation that seems to suit you.
10. Seek specialized evaluation through tests of personality, aptitude and intelligence.
11. Seek the Lord's guidance.

These major areas can be evaluated in several counseling sessions. As a young person begins to understand his assets and liabilities, he can better understand the guidance of the Lord into a vocation appropriate for him. God does not give a person gifts to be wasted in the wrong profession. He distributes to each one the abilities necessary to do the tasks to which he is called. By understanding his strengths, he can better come to the place of service which the Lord has planned for him.

HOMESICKNESS

Among younger children the problem of anxiety over separation from parents is very common. The homesick child can run the gamut from mild feelings of apprehension to severe outbreaks of crying and uncontrolled emotion.

A new and threatening experience is the overt environmental cause of homesickness. Everyone who enters into a totally new experience has some feelings of inquisitiveness or apprehension. Even well-adjusted people feel a tinge of anxiety when taking an important examination or applying for a new job. When an insecure child faces a new situation he is more easily threatened than others and may react with overt signs of homesickness or a desire to return to a more secure environment.

Separation from friends and loved ones is another basic factor. A camp experience or any new situation may remove the child from his source of emotional support and gratification. This leaves him susceptible to many conflicts and anxieties.

The older child who becomes fearful and upset when

separated from his home may be an *insecure individual.* He is frequently *overly dependent.* Such a child has often been overprotected by his parents. He has not been allowed or encouraged to develop a sense of dependency. He becomes fearful of his inability to function without support and guidance.

Fear of rejection is frequently a factor in instances of homesickness. The child who has been unloved and rejected in the home may come to expect rejection. Although he receives little affection at home, he fears leaving since he may lose what little emotional gratification he does have. When placed in a new environment he becomes upset because he is sensitive to any lack of acceptance. Whereas the normal child learns to interact and enjoy a new situation, the insecure person is constantly afraid of rejection and rebuff.

Specific fears or traumatic experiences are sometimes responsible for homesickness. Some children have been separated from their parents when one family member experienced a severe illness or injury. Such illness or a death provides a realistic fear for a child to be separated from loved ones. Although this is a rare cause of homesickness, it is often the most difficult to resolve since the fear is so realistically based in a traumatic life experience.

Lack of preparation for separation from parents can add to feelings of insecurity. When a child is adequately prepared for a new experience, he can understand and accept it without fear. By talking over the new environment to be faced, the sense of newness and threat diminishes. The child gains a sense of security in his knowledge. Without this preparation a child is more likely to experience fear and apprehension.

In dealing with a homesick child, it is important to *make him feel at home.* Since this problem centers upon feelings of anxiety over separation from loved ones, you should make the child feel secure and an important member of the group. When this is accomplished you remove much of the basis of the difficulty.

Another important concept in working with a homesick child is to *keep him busy.* Feelings of apprehension and fearfulness most frequently show up at times when the child is alone and not participating in an activity. Free periods and near bedtime are commonly associated with heightened feelings of homesickness. When a child is occupied with interesting activities, he has less opportunity to concern himself with his feelings of loneliness. As a camp counselor you need to spot these children early, and make every effort to see that they are engaged in the activities of the day. This preventative measure is one of the most important steps in avoiding the problem of homesickness.

A counselor can frequently *be a substitute parent*. Since the child's fears may center upon separation from his parents, you should try to meet this emotional need. The insecure child wants someone to turn to with his problems — someone who will listen and understand. He needs an adult who will not scold or reject him because he is afraid and insecure. Keep an eye on this child, and be ready with much comfort and assurance. This will give him the added support necessary to meet the demands of this new and threatening experience.

You should also *talk to the child about his homesickness*. Don't go overboard and emphasize the problem, or you may only make it worse. But you can help the child to understand his feelings. By encouraging him to discuss his problem, you can gain understanding of the sources of his difficulty. By quietly reassuring him, you can help relieve the symptoms of fear and worry. One important concept that you can discuss with this child is that some homesickness is normal. Most children have feelings of apprehension when they first begin to leave their parents. By seeing that he is not alone in the problem, an insecure child gains increased security and confidence. You can also help him to understand why he is afraid. With older children this is especially beneficial. As you discuss the causes of homesickness, the older child can understand that his fear is based upon his need for support from his parents and his own lack of confidence in his ability.* This knowledge of the cause of the problem assists the child to overcome his fear.

An understanding of God's love and protection is a great source of security for the fearful and anxious child. A mother recently related an experience of her young daughter. She told

---

*For a discussion of the dynamics of insecurity and a plan of therapy for older children and adults, see the author's book, *Encyclopedia of Psychological Problems*.

how the girl had been unable to sleep and was very fearful the night before. The mother asked the daughter why she had not called for her to come. This young girl replied, "I didn't want to wake you, Mother, so I just started saying Scripture I had memorized. When I came to that verse 'What time I am afraid, I will trust in thee' (Psalm 56:3), I went off to sleep." And how true this is. The Word of God is a powerful resource for every believer. When a child is afraid, one of the most significant contributions you can make is to lead him to a greater understanding of God's love and keeping care over His own.

Lying

Any person working with children and youth soon comes into contact with instances of lying and deceit. This problem is frequently misunderstood because it seems to be entirely a spiritual one. The Scripture is clear that lying is sin. "Lie not one to another, seeing that ye have put off the old man with his deeds; And have put on the new man, which is renewed in knowledge after the image of him that created him" (Colossians 3:9, 10). But because we are quick to recognize the spiritual aspect of the problem, a counselor may be prone to merely tell the person to ask forgiveness and not to lie again. Such treatment may not deal with all the basic causes of the disturbance. Most lies are not simply a matter of trying to be disobedient to God, although they are definitely that. Lying can have definite emotional causes which must be understood if the underlying problem is to be overcome.

Most children at times exaggerate information. This is quite common and, unless carried to a serious degree, need be no great cause for concern. The child who exaggerates needs to be corrected and helped to see that his statements are inaccurate. This can often be done very easily since there is not a serious underlying problem.

A common form of lying is *the defensive lie.* When a child is faced with the possibility of punishment or correction, he may shape information in order to avoid the consequences of his actions. Parents sometimes contribute to this pattern by punishing a child every time they find he transgresses a set standard. The child soon learns that his parents will not allow him to discuss the problem and try to overcome it. The only way to avoid punishment is to lie and conceal the truth.

Children who have *serious feelings of inferiority* may create false stories in order to gain the approval of others. Feeling unworthy and rejected by others, this person thinks he can impress others if he tells some interesting story of his own accomplishments.

The insecure and jealous person may create a lie about another person in order to express feelings of hostility and resentment. Wanting to attack another person, but being too fearful, the jealous person may start a rumor about his enemy which is his attempt to get revenge.

When a person is continually lying and being deceitful, he is apt to be suffering from a *serious personality disturbance*. The delinquent or anti-social personality is often found to have a consistent pattern of deceit. The teen-ager who steals and drinks must cover his actions with false accounts of his activities if he is to avoid punishment.*

A lack of spiritual conversion and growth is another basic factor in deceit. The unregenerate soul is controlled by the sin nature. It is natural for him to lie and seek his own pleasures. The carnal Christian may also have much difficulty with lying. Without the continual control of the Holy Spirit, every person is prone to fall into sin. When one lives apart from the Lord, these difficulties are to be expected.

In dealing with a deceitful child, it is important to realize that this is a symptom of his real problem. Lying is an attempt to adjust to certain internal and external forces. It is an attempt to resolve the conflicts between one's internal deeds and the demands of society.

A judgmental attitude should be avoided. One of the causes of lying is often the fact that the child is trying to hide something from a critical authority figure. If you take this same authoritative role, the child is likely to react to you with the same deceit as he does to others.

As a counselor, you can *help the inferior person realize that his lying is an attempt to prove to others his adequacy.* Then you can help him to see that he is a worthy person with good

---

*For a discussion of the problem of delinquency see the author's book, *Encyclopedia of Psychological Problems*.

abilities. He does not have to lie and scheme in order to be accepted. If he will be himself and evidence a good degree of adjustment and love for the Lord, others will turn to him and accept him into the group.

The person who lies will not likely change his behavior unless he comes to *a clear understanding of the causes of his problem.* You can help here by raising questions such as, "Why do you think some persons learn to be deceitful?" or, "How do you think your feelings of inferiority influence your lying?" This person must see that lying doesn't just happen. There is a reason — and it can be found. Once it is found it can be overcome.

The greatest resource for overcoming any sin problem lies in *the forgiveness of God and the consequent power of the Holy Spirit to control the life of the believer.* After your counselee gains an understanding of the basic causes of his problem, you can lead him to ask the forgiveness of God. As he walks in closer fellowship with Christ, he has all of the resources of God at his disposal to turn back any future temptation to deceive others through false speech. A strong program of Christian fellowship, Bible study, prayer and witnessing is of utmost importance in developing the walk with Christ which will overcome the sinful nature and allow a walk in accordance with the desires of the Lord.

PARENTAL CONFLICT

Many young people have conflicts with their parents. Some are minor, others are serious. A measure of parental conflict is to be expected. Youth are developing and becoming more independent. They are preparing to "leave the nest" and strike out on their own. They must begin to think and provide for themselves.

The causes of some conflicts are evident. For instance, both parents may be saved, but the son (or daughter) may not be. Only one of the parents may be a believer. Perhaps just the young person knows Christ. Such conditions produce conflicts because the saved and the unsaved naturally think and act differently.

Conflicts may develop during the teen years because the parents have not established a good relationship with the child in the preadolescent years. Now the boy wishes to assert himself. Dad, though, isn't ready for this. Almost any independent action is considered as rebellion. As a result, the youth feels deep resentment toward his parent. He has reached a virtual impasse — the "end of the road" — so to speak.

So, he comes to you with his problems. And you — with God's guidance — can help him. Here are some ways:

Encourage the counselee to talk about his problems. Draw him out and listen to him. Let him ventilate his feelings and resentments. If you do nothing but listen, you will have helped him. Once he gets his conflicts out into the open, out of himself where he can see them, they often have a way of becoming smaller or disappearing.

Even though you may be able to do little about his home conditions, simply being a willing listener will be of tremendous service. He may never have talked to anyone at length about his problems. This is where you can help him.

As a counselor, help him consider the causes of his conflicts. Help him understand why his parents feel as they do. In a sense, encourage him to step, for example, into his dad's shoes — to view things as a father, husband and provider. You do young people no favor when you pit them against their parents. The knowledge and skills which boys and girls gain in learning to get along with parents can serve them well throughout life in getting along with anyone — young or old.

Try, also, to help the young person understand his own attitudes. He will probably not find solutions to his problems until he verbalizes and understands the causes of his difficulties.

On the basis of the above information, you can make practical solutions. For example, you might ask, "Are you communicating with your parents?" Ask him also if he is recognizing his parents' feelings? After all, Mother isn't the "queen of the campus" anymore, and Dad's health problems and financial strains may be causing him serious concerns. A few sincere compliments from a son or daughter mean much to parents.

At this point you might ask Jim if he's been careful about cleaning his room, or if he has been "dropping things where they come off" and letting Mother pick them up. Or Mary might be questioned about her share of the cooking or cleaning. Have they been expecting personal valet service from Mother? And a personal bank account with Dad?

Very possibly, the young person hasn't thought of these matters as being contributing factors in his personal resentments and conflicts. As a counselor, you can enable youth to see themselves. You can encourage them to go home with different attitudes toward their parents.

Another way you can help youth is to *lead them into a deeper and richer devotional life.* Even if the home situation cannot be revolutionized, the young person's new attitude will make it a better place than before. Even if the parents cannot be changed, your counselee *can* be, which might make all the difference in the world.

If your counselee is not a Christian, you can affect a miracle in his life by leading him to Jesus Christ. If he is a believer, you can help him grow in the things of the Lord. You can point out that whereas he might have been attempting to solve all his problems in his own strength, he can take them to the Lord. And there he can find victory. Read together the Apostle Paul's words: "I can do all things through Christ which strengtheneth me" (Philippians 4:13). Indicate that the words — "all things" — *include getting along with parents.*

SEX PROBLEMS

A counselor will be confronted with many sex problems as he deals with young people. As a counselor reflects on the nature of sex, he understands why sexual maladjustments arise:

1. Sex problems grow out of the fact that sexual drives are persistent, dynamic forces in life.
2. Some sex problems arise because sexual adjustments are a reflection of, and have an influence on, various aspects of one's total personality.
3. Sex problems and adjustments often stem from the wide variation in sex drives.
4. Many sex problems come from lack of wholesome sex education.
5. Faulty childhood impressions and unwise handling by parents have profound effects, sometimes causing sex problems later in life.

6. Organic abnormalities may be causitive in sex problems, predisposing one toward maladjustments.
7. Since sex acts often result in human reproduction, many serious problems may follow.
8. Sex problems are sometimes created and/or aggravated by a secular society which places unusual emphasis on sex.
9. Spiritual factors (lack of spiritual devotion) are important in cases of sexual maladjustment.

Often sex problems are not really sex problems. That is, they are seldom organic, or physical. As you counsel with young people, you will find that sex problems stem from personality disturbances, adjustment difficulties or spiritual problems. Consequently, when you consider sex problems, give attention to the total personality of the young person. Consider his major life conflicts, and do not overlook the spiritual aspects of his problems. Very often when you help a person to develop spiritually, and encourage him to walk closely with the Lord, his sex problems are resolved.

Although young people may present a variety of sex problems, there are several that are brought to the counselor's attention most frequently.

Masturbation

Masturbation is the self-stimulation of the sex organs, resulting in an orgasm. In adolescence new hormonal activity begins, producing sexual tension and desires which can be relieved through masturbation.

This is a problem which bothers many young people. Occasional self-stimulation of the genitals during childhood, and masturbation during adolescence is quite common. It is not unusual for unmarried individuals to gain some sexual satisfaction and release by this means.

Insecure children will often attempt to gain gratification and relief from tension through masturbation, somewhat in the same manner that they would turn to nail biting or thumb sucking. When a child masturbates compulsively there is usually an underlying disturbance which is causing this behavior.

Another dynamic, frequently underlying chronic masturbation, is the feeling of sexual inadequacy. By masturbating the young person consciously or unconsciously attempts to prove to himself that he is capable of normal sexual functioning.

When young people continue to masturbate excessively, rather than to develop normal heterosexual behavior, it is usually a sign of maladjustment.

Counseling with individuals who masturbate excessively should be directed toward understanding basic factors which have led to this type of behavior. Merely telling a person who masturbates that the habit is bad or sinful is no solution. What is needed, rather, is an understanding of the causes of the problem. This may require several counseling sessions.

The counselee must come to an understanding of the factors responsible for his feelings of insecurity, if this is his basic problem. As he begins to comprehend and discuss them, he will develop increased confidence and he will be better able to develop normal sexual patterns.

Sex education is another important consideration in counseling with young people who masturbate frequently. These persons may have various misconceptions concerning sexual functioning. The counselor needs to help them develop normal, wholesome attitudes toward the human body if he is to enable them to overcome their sexual maladjustments.

Self-control comes, also, from a dedicated life in Christ. As you challenge a young person to yield to the Lord and to become involved in Christian work, God will give control and victory. Such consecration is a matter of steady growth over a period of time.

Homosexuality

The development of adult heterosexuality (normal attitudes and desires toward the opposite sex) is a long and complex process. Because of the numerous factors which influence this development, many people fail to achieve normal sexual adjustment. Homosexuality is characterized by an unnatural sex attraction for members of one's own sex. Although the term "homosexuality" may apply to either sex, the term "lesbianism" applies to women only.

Some very masculine appearing men and some women with

very feminine appearances are engaged in homosexual activities. The homosexual is a person who is afraid of normal involvement with the opposite sex. Fearing this contact, he turns to members of his own sex in order to receive gratification.

Various theories have been given concerning the origin of homosexuality, but it is now widely agreed that this disorder is largely the result of abnormal personality development. A number of conditions may contribute to this deviation.

Glandular Disturbances: Some researchers give important consideration to hormonal causes of homosexuality. However, several factors minimize the importance of such an endocrine imbalance: (1) All homosexuals do not exhibit these imbalances, (2) many people who are not homosexuals exhibit similar disturbances, and (3) individuals have made changes from homosexual behavior to normal heterosexual adjustments without altering this glandular imbalance.

Dominant Mother: Some mothers stifle and belittle their son's masculinity. When this happens the child loses confidence in his own sex. A dominant mother may have a strong, masculine component in her personality and may rival her son for the father's affection. This development is often on an unconscious level. As the son loses confidence in his masculinity, he may dread the thought of marriage or any intimacy with women.

Weak Father: When a dominant mother is paired with a weak father, an unhealthy situation is intensified. The son cannot look to his father for moral support in his desire to become a man. He may then lose respect for his father and his own sex. A daughter may lose respect for men in general because of her father's weakness.

Overindulgent Mother: The overindulgent mother is also a common causative factor in homosexuality. Her indulgence leads the boy to develop a strong attachment to his mother which he is unable to break as he grows older. He feels that no girl can measure up to his mother and he does not develop normal heterosexual friendships.

Cruel Parents: A mother or father who is continually cruel and arbitrary may cause the child of the opposite sex to develop ill feelings toward others of the same sex as the cruel parent. These hostile feelings result in the inability to establish adequate heterosexual relationships and lead the person to find gratification and acceptance from those of his own sex.

Overly Close Relationship With a Parent of the Same Sex: When a young child has an extremely intimate relationship with one parent, to the exclusion of normal identification with the other, the child is unable to develop healthy heterosexual attitudes. Since the child's early experiences have been almost totally with the parent of the same sex, he is unable to relate to those of the opposite sex.

In a godless, secular society it is not surprising that men and women have turned to all types of sexual activity. In Romans 1:24-27, we read of the sinful behavior resulting from the rejection of God: "Therefore God gave them up in the lusts of their [own] hearts to sexual impurity, to the dishonoring of their bodies among themselves, abandoning them to the degrading power of sin. Because they exchanged the truth of God for a lie and worshipped and served the creature rather than the Creator, Who is blessed forever! Amen — so be it. For this reason God gave them over *and* abandoned them to vile affections *and* degrading passions. For their women exchanged their natural function for an unnatural and abnormal one; And the men also turned from natural relations with women and were set ablaze (burned out, consumed) with lust for one another, men committing shameful acts with men and suffering in their own bodies *and* personalities the inevitable consequences *and* penalty of their wrong doing and going astray, which was [their] fitting retribution" (*Amplified Bible*).

Homosexuality is one result of the apostasy of the world and sinful man's refusal to worship God.

Since the homosexual's difficulties arise in connection with an inability to relate properly to others, it is important that the counselor provide an accepting, non-critical atmosphere for the counselee. The homosexual has had inadequate relationships with significant adults in his environment. One of the major factors which will assist him to overcome his misdirected sexual drives will be the formation of a clearer role concept based upon his new relationship with the therapist. As he begins to relate to the counselor, he can gradually form correct attitudes toward his sexual role. It may be a long-term process, but the counselor can help the homosexual to understand the dynamics of his disorder.*

A strong program of spiritual development for the believer and a genuine conversion for the unsaved are of utmost importance in overcoming serious sexual problems. Experienced Christian counselors know that many are not seriously concerned about their problem until they have been spiritually converted. After one trusts in Christ as his personal Savior, he is convicted by the Holy Spirit for his abnormal sexual practices and he knows his actions are not pleasing to God. This usually causes him to be concerned about his condition and prompts him to seek professional help.

Spiritual growth not only convicts a man of his abnormal sexual activities, but it also enables him to overcome them. This recovery is clearly spoken of in the sixth chapter of I Corinthians: "Do you not know that the unrighteous *and* the wrongdoers will not inherit *or* have any share in the kingdom of God? Do not be deceived (misled); neither the impure *and* immoral, nor idolators, nor adulterers, nor those who participate in homosexuality." In the 11th verse we find that those people spoken of in the 9th verse *overcame* their homosexuality. "And such some of you were (once). But you were washed clean [purified by a complete atonement for sin and made free from the guilt of sin]; and you were consecrated (set apart, hallowed); and you were justified (pronounced righteous, by trust) in the name of the Lord Jesus Christ and in the (Holy) Spirit of our God" (I Corinthians 6:9-11, *Amplified Bible*).

When Christ controls one's life, He controls his sexual appetite as well. A man may lust after another man sexually. *But he need not* any more than a man would lust after a woman. In other words, a man engaged in homosexuality may not be able to magically change all the dynamics of his childhood, but he *can* call on the Lord to control him and to change him. There is no more justification for a man to lust after a man than for a man to lust after a woman. Both can utilize the power of God. In the second chapter of Ephesians, verses one through five, God tells us that whereas a man once walked according to the

---

*For a detailed discussion of this topic, see the author's book, *Encyclopedia of Psychological Problems*.

course of this world, fulfilling the desires of the flesh and of the mind, through Christ he is *quickened* — made alive with new power from God, Himself. If a counselor can lead a person into a close walk with the Lord, He will set up a standard against the former lusts and abnormal practices and help him to be an overcomer.

SPIRITUAL PROBLEMS

Counseling with children and young people involves many spiritual problems. Some know about Christ, but do not know Him personally as Savior. Still others lack the assurance of salvation. As young children they may have received the Savior, but now they do not have the assurance of eternal life. Many young people are in a backslidden condition. They need to be restored to the joy of living for Chirst. Others know they are saved, but they are at a standstill. They need a program for spiritual growth and development. Some young people, especially those who have been recently saved or have dedicated their lives to Christ, need help in facing parents and friends. Their recent stand for Christ may be seriously handicapped unless they learn the secrets of victorious living.

Counseling With the Unsaved

Becky was a high school junior. She was sharp, but unsaved. During the summer she attended a high school camp. It was evident that she needed to know the Savior. There are many like Becky whose greatest need is counseling about their lost condition.

Your greatest contribution in life can be counseling and winning souls to the Lord. You may do many other things, but the greatest, surely, is the winning of young lives to Christ. Counselors should be alert to every opportunity to point young people to the Savior.

How can boys and girls be won? First, gain their confidence. Let them know you are interested in them. Second, encourage them to talk about how they feel. Third, present the simple plan of salvation:

1. You need to be saved (Romans 3:23).
2. You can't save yourself (Ephesians 2:8, 9).

3. Christ can save you (I Timothy 2:5, 6; Hebrews 7:25; John 3:16).
4. Call upon the Lord (Romans 10:13).
5. He gives you assurance (John 10:28).

Ask your counselee to simply pray and ask Christ to come into his heart. You may want him to repeat a prayer after you. Then encourage him to tell someone about his decision. Give him a verse of Scripture to memorize, and follow him up as often as possible.

Counseling Those Who Lack the Assurance of Salvation

Some may have received the Lord as Savior when they were very young, but now they are unsure. Others may have raised their hand in a meeting, or prayed, but now they are confused about the matter.

Counseling with such young people can enable them to be *sure*. It will give them the confidence they need to grow. Further, it will help them to witness to others. When a person is sure of his salvation he is free to live victoriously for Christ.

Verses that are helpful in dealing with youth who are unsure of their salvation are I John 5:11-13; and John 5:24.

Counseling With Young People Who Are Backslidden

These are believers who are not living in fellowship with their Lord. Daily living makes it easy for Christian young people to become involved with the unsaved — then fall into sin. Such was Jane, who was placed in a school for girls, where she came to know Christ. But when she was released, she went back with the old gang and soon was slipping away from the Lord. Then she was invited to go to camp where she found friends who really cared about her. How may Jane and others be restored? Encourage backslidden young people to admit their sin. Help them to reason through the causes of their falling away. When they are aware of the causes, they can see how to overcome them in the future. These Scripture verses are especially helpful: I John 1:9; Psalm 51:12, 13.

Counseling Youth to Grow Spiritually

Many young people are not growing in the things of the Lord. They have no program for development. Actually everyone should have a plan for growing and becoming mature Christians. Young people need more than the counselor's Bible verse and prayer. They need a program. You can encourage your counselee to: (1) read the Bible daily, (2) develop a regular, strong prayer life, (3) seek out and cultivate Christian friendships, (4) attend a Bible-believing church, (5) read Christian books and listen to Christian music, (6) witness to others.

As you counsel with boys and girls, point out the fact that Christian maturity is the result of planned, continuous growth. You might use an illustration such as this: "A man bought two young, identical vines. He planted one just outside his kitchen door, and the other some distance from his house — at the far edge of the backyard. Two years later he noticed that the vine far from the house was sickly-looking and stunted. But the vine next to the kitchen door was green, vigorous, covered with blossoms, and so large that it had to be trimmed frequently. Then he learned what had happened. The vine at the edge of the yard seldom received any water. But the family, in putting the empty milk bottles on the porch of the kitchen each day, always filled the bottles with water and emptied them on the nearby vine. So it is with you and me. As we receive spiritual nourishment *each day*, we will grow into strong, mature Christians."

Counseling About Returning to a Non-Christian Environment

One of the most saddening experiences of a Christian worker is seeing a young person accept Christ as Savior, then returning home and losing his vital faith in the Lord. But this happens repeatedly. A person finds Christ at church or camp, but the new-found life is sometimes lost in the routine of daily living.

Some boys and girls lose out spiritually because their *parents do not know Christ as Savior*. The parents do not recognize the value of spiritual things and are unable to encourage their children. As a result many young people do not begin regular attendance at church services and youth activities. Since they are receiving no spiritual food, they are vulnerable to the attacks of Satan.

Old friends are one of the greatest hindrances to the spiritual growth of believers. When a person returns to the old gang, he is likely to compromise his new-found faith. In order to be accepted by the group, he plays along with secular ideals and activities. The Scripture gives clear admonitions such as, "Blessed is the man that walketh not in the counsel of the ungodly, nor standeth in the way of sinners, nor sitteth in the seat of the scornful" (Psalm 1:1). Also, "Can two walk together, except they be agreed?" (Amos 3:3).

Old habits from the unconverted life have a strong pull on the new Christian. Satan is active and makes ready use of smoking, swearing, drinking, dancing and other things in trying to keep a young person from total surrender to Christ. Unless these habits are overcome, the new Christian will continue to lead a frustrated and defeated life.

If the new Christian is to grow rapidly, he must be prepared to meet these negative influences such as family, friends and habits. He must also have a positive program of spiritual development.

You can *frankly discuss with the counselee the unhealthy influence of unsaved friends and worldly activities.* The knowledge of this potential danger will enable the new Christian to steer away from unhealthy influences and seek more wholesome friendships and activities.

The positive side of the Christian life is even more important. If a person has a strong love for the Lord, and is growing in the faith, the Lord will give the power to weed worldly influences out of his life. Without the motivating power of the Holy Spirit, all efforts to change are simply self-improvement and reform. They are no more spiritually important than the high moral and ethical standards of many unsaved individuals.

Prayer is the initial key to the Christian life. Every believer has the need and privilege to speak to the Lord. In counseling with a new believer, you can discuss the basic elements of prayer such as adoration, praise and thanksgiving, intercession for others and personal petition. By stressing the importance of a well-rounded prayer life, you are encouraging the new Christian to utilize the most potent force in the world.

It is not enough for the new Christian to speak *to* the Lord. He must allow the Lord to speak to him. This is the place of *daily Bible study.* As we read the Bible, the Lord speaks to us through His inspired Word. Without an increasing knowledge of the Bible, the Christian life grows stale and stagnant. There is little growth or victory.

Fellowship with other Christians is another important ingredient in the growing Christian's life. He needs the spiritual encouragement and support received when he shares with other believers. So talk to him about church attendance. Help him find fellowship in a Bible-believing church which has an active program for his age group.

One of the most thrilling experiences of any Christian is to *share the good news of God's love with another.* As a counselor, you can help the new Christian to memorize some basic verses outlining the plan of salvation. With a few Scripture verses and an awareness of what Christ has done for him personally, a new Christian is able to witness. Of course, he may not know the answers to many questions, but his own testimony and the basic plan of salvation are enough to win others. You may be able to suggest a gospel team from a local church or Christian organization.

There are many different ways of witnessing: (a) By distributing tracts, (b) by sharing Christian books and magazines, (c) by cooperating with youth organizations interested in soul winning, (d) by taking a person to church where he can hear the Gospel, (e) by talking personally to others about Christ.

The opportunity to share what Christ means to him is a wonderful thrill for the Christian. Witnessing will not only help a person to grow; it will also keep him from sin.

Christians have access to many aids to spiritual growth. There are literally hundreds of *outstanding books.* Bible study aids, devotionals and biographies of outstanding men and women of God can have a tremendous influence on the life of a believer. *Christian music, films and magazines* are packed with vital material for the new and growing believer. You do a great service when you show your counselee how he can utilize these resources as supplements to a solid program of prayer, Bible study and witnessing.

In summarizing a plan of spiritual growth for new Christians, the following major points are important: (1) Personal resources of prayer, Bible study and witnessing, (2) the influence of Christian fellowship in a local church and with other believers of similar age, (3) the need for preparation against harmful effects of old friends, old habits and old entertainment. If these major areas are considered, the new Christian should be well on his way toward a growing and meaningful relationship with Jesus Christ.

WITHDRAWAL AND SHYNESS

The quiet, timid individual is usually not recognized as suffering from emotional problems since he is no disturbance to the group. Whereas the rebellious person is disruptive and belligerent, the shy person doesn't bother others. He minds his own business, and his problems may go unnoticed for many years. But professional people realize that the withdrawn person is often the one with the most serious problems. Rather than working out his conflicts and frustrations, he blames himself. He may become increasingly withdrawn and develop strong feelings of guilt, unworthiness and depression. As he grows older, this person lacks self-confidence. He finds difficulty in living a victorious Christian life because he constantly feels depressed and defeated. He is unable to enjoy the experiences of life, and may need long-term professional care to overcome lifelong patterns of withdrawal.

Parents of withdrawn children are themselves often shy and seclusive. When adults are fearful and insecure, they impart this sense of inadequacy to their children. Thus a young person grows up feeling that life's experiences are too overwhelming to meet. Instead they must be avoided with fear and withdrawal.

Individuals who have overprotective parents often develop a behavioral pattern characterized by seclusion and withdrawal. In their well-meaning behavior, the parents have failed to allow the child to develop a sense of confidence and independence. Since the parents met the young person's every need, he did not have to stand on his own. Now, years later, he is faced with a new responsibility for which he is totally unprepared. He is accustomed to turning to mother or dad for support and guidance, and without this help he must retreat from the frustrating situation.

Children who experience little or no love or security in their homes, find it difficult to develop social interactions with others outside the home. It is with parents and relatives that we first learn to develop social skills and confidence. When a child is criticized and rejected in this environment, he finds himself unable to react normally in other situations. His confidence and security have been undermined by the lack of love, affection and security at home.

Occasionally a child has failed to develop adequate social interaction, basically because of the *lack of opportunity for social contacts*. Children raised in rural areas with no playmates may later suffer from lessened confidence in interpersonal relationships.

When you are working with a shy youngster, you can be of much assistance by trying many means to develop his sense of confidence and security. *Abundant praise and opportunities to achieve success in simple tasks lead to greater confidence in future undertakings.* By supporting and encouraging the insecure child to take a part in a social situation where he can be successful, you avoid another failure and give a real opportunity to increase his feelings of adequacy.

If you are able to *talk with the parents of an insecure and withdrawn child*, they can be helped to understand his need for acceptance, praise and security. As parents begin to meet the child's emotional needs, he will respond with an improved sense of self-confidence and lessened withdrawal.

In counseling with a young person who is concerned over his shyness and withdrawal, you have a tremendous ministry. You can *help the person discuss his feelings of insecurity and inferiority and then gradually recognize their causes.* As he begins to see the relationship between past experiences and his current withdrawal, you can help him develop a new sense of confidence and security. This will overcome the tendency to withdraw from social settings.

Young people who are withdrawn can find unlimited help through *spiritual means*. As they trust in Christ and grow in the faith, they can develop a self-concept which is supportive and helpful. There is a wonderful confidence which comes with the knowledge that one is a child of God and an object of His love. As your counselee begins to study the Scriptures, he will come to realize that God is always with him and anxious to meet his needs. This assurance brings much confidence and gives the strength to overcome feelings of insecurity and resultant withdrawal.

QUESTIONS FOR DISCUSSION

1. If a young person asks you to promise that you will not tell anyone what he is about to tell you, should you make the promise?
2. List several ways in which a person may reveal his aggression and hostility.
3. Why do some boys and girls go to extremes to gain attention?
4. At approximately what age do most children achieve bladder control?
5. What are some of the most frequent questions young people ask about dating?
6. List several causes of extreme dress and inappropriate grooming.
7. List several advantages of attending Bible schools and Christian colleges.
8. What steps might a counselor take if a child or young person says he is homesick?
9. List several possible causes of lying.
10. Why is it important for a counselor to strengthen relationships between a teen-ager and his parents?
11. List several basic understandings which you have gained from the discussion of sex.
12. What is meant by a program of spiritual development? What does it consist of?
13. How can a counselor help a counselee to overcome his withdrawn tendencies and shyness?
14. What, in your opinion, were several of the significant contributions of this chapter?

7

Selected Scripture for Use in Counseling

ADULTERY

Exodus 20:14

Thou shalt not commit adultery.

Proverbs 6:27-33

Can a man take fire in his bosom, and his clothes not be burned? Can one go upon hot coals, and his feet not be burned? So he that goeth in to his neighbour's wife; whosoever toucheth her shall not be innocent. Men do not despise a thief, if he steal to satisfy his soul when he is hungry; But if he be found, he shall restore sevenfold; he shall give all the substance of his house. But whoso committeth adultery with a woman lacketh understanding: he that doeth it destroyeth his own soul. A wound and dishonour shall he get; and his reproach shall not be wiped away.

Matthew 5:28

But I say unto you, That whosoever looketh on a woman to lust after her hath committed adultery with her already in his heart.

ANXIETY AND WORRY

Philippians 4:6, 7

Be careful for nothing; but in every thing by prayer and supplication with thanksgiving let your requests be made known unto God. And the peace of God, which passeth all understanding, shall keep your hearts and minds through Christ Jesus.

Philippians 4:19

But my God shall supply all your need according to his riches in glory by Christ Jesus.

I Peter 5:7

Casting all your care upon him; for he careth for you.

ASSURANCE OF SALVATION

John 5:24

Verily, verily, I say unto you, He that heareth my word, and believeth on him that sent me, hath everlasting life, and shall not come into condemnation; but is passed from death unto life.

John 6:37

All that the Father giveth me shall come to me; and him that cometh to me I will in no wise cast out.

John 10:28

And I give unto them eternal life; and they shall never perish, neither shall any man pluck them out of my hand.

I John 5:13

These things have I written unto you that believe on the name of the Son of God; that ye may know that ye have eternal life.

BEREAVEMENT AND LOSS

Deuteronomy 31:8

And the LORD, he it is that doth go before thee; he will be with thee, he will not fail thee, neither forsake thee: fear not, neither be dismayed.

Psalm 27:10
When my father and my mother forsake me, then the LORD will take me up.

II Corinthians 6:10
As sorrowful, yet always rejoicing; as poor, yet making many rich; as having nothing, yet possessing all things.

COMFORT
Psalm 23:4
Yea, though I walk through the valley of the shadow of death, I will fear no evil: for thou art with me; thy rod and thy staff they comfort me.

Matthew 5:4
Blessed are they that mourn: for they shall be comforted.

Matthew 11:28
Come unto me, all ye that labour and are heavy laden, and I will give you rest.

II Corinthians 1:3, 4
Blessed be God, even the Father of our Lord Jesus Christ, the Father of mercies, and the God of all comfort; Who comforteth us in all our tribulation, that we may be able to comfort them which are in any trouble, by the comfort wherewith we ourselves are comforted of God.

CONFIDENCE (Developing)
Proverbs 3:26
For the LORD shall be thy confidence, and shall keep thy foot from being taken.

Proverbs 14:26
In the fear of the LORD is strong confidence: and his children shall have a place of refuge.

Galatians 6:9
And let us not be weary in well doing: for in due season we shall reap, if we faint not.

Philippians 4:13
I can do all things through Christ which strengtheneth me.

I Peter 2:9
But ye are a chosen generation, a royal priesthood, an holy nation, a peculiar people; that ye should shew forth the praises of him who hath called you out of darkness into his marvellous light.

DANGER (Protection from)
Psalm 32:7
Thou art my hiding place; thou shalt preserve me from trouble; thou shalt compass me about with songs of deliverance.

Psalm 34:7
The angel of the LORD encampeth round about them that fear him, and delivereth them.

Psalm 34:17
The righteous cry, and the LORD heareth, and delivereth them out of all their troubles.

Psalm 91:1
He that dwelleth in the secret place of the most High shall abide under the shadow of the Almighty.

Psalm 91:11
For he shall give his angels charge over thee, to keep thee in all thy ways.

Romans 14:8
For whether we live, we live unto the Lord; and whether we die, we die unto the Lord: whether we live therefore, or die, we are the Lord's.

DEATH
Psalm 116:15
Precious in the sight of the LORD is the death of his saints.

Lamentations 3:32, 33
But though he cause grief, yet will he have compassion according to the multitude of his mercies. For he doth not afflict willingly nor grieve the children of men.

Philippians 1:21
For me to live is Christ, and to die is gain.

DIFFICULTIES (Discipline through)

Romans 8:28

And we know that all things work together for good to them that love God, to them who are the called according to his purpose.

Hebrews 12:7

If ye endure chastening, God dealeth with you as with sons; for what son is he whom the father chasteneth not?

Revelation 3:19

And as many as I love, I rebuke and chasten: be zealous therefore, and repent.

DISAPPOINTMENT

Psalm 55:22

Cast thy burden upon the LORD, and he shall sustain thee: he shall never suffer the righteous to be moved.

II Corinthians 4:8, 9

We are troubled on every side, yet not distressed; we are perplexed, but not in despair; Persecuted, but not forsaken; cast down, but not destroyed.

DISCOURAGEMENT

Joshua 1:9

Have not I commanded thee? Be strong and of a good courage; be not afraid, neither be thou dismayed: for the LORD thy God is with thee whithersoever thou goest.

Psalm 27:14

Wait on the LORD: be of good courage, and he shall strengthen thine heart: wait, I say, on the LORD.

John 16:33

These things I have spoken unto you, that in me ye might have peace. In the world ye shall have tribulation: but be of good cheer; I have overcome the world.

FAITH

Romans 10:17

So then faith cometh by hearing, and hearing by the word of God.

Ephesians 2:8, 9

For by grace are ye saved through faith; and that not of yourselves: it is the gift of God: Not of works, lest any man should boast.

Hebrews 11:1

Now faith is the substance of things hoped for, the evidence of things not seen.

Hebrews 11:6

But without faith it is impossible to please him: for he that cometh to God must believe that he is, and that he is a rewarder of them that diligently seek him.

James 1:5, 6

If any of you lack wisdom, let him ask of God, that giveth to all men liberally, and upbraideth not; and it shall be given him. But let him ask in faith, nothing wavering. For he that wavereth is like a wave of the sea driven with the wind and tossed.

FEAR

Psalm 27:1

The LORD is my light and my salvation; whom shall I fear? the LORD is the strength of my life; of whom shall I be afraid?

Romans 8:31

What shall we then say to these things? If God be for us, who can be against us?

II Timothy 1:7

For God hath not given us the spirit of fear; but of power, and of love, and of a sound mind.

FORGIVENESS OF SIN

Psalm 32:5

I acknowledged my sin unto thee, and mine iniquity have I not hid. I said, I will confess my transgressions unto the LORD; and thou forgavest the iniquity of my sin.

Psalm 51 (all)

Proverbs 28:13

He that covereth his sins shall not prosper: but whoso confesseth and forsaketh them shall have mercy.

Isaiah 1:18
Come now, and let us reason together, saith the LORD: though your sins be as scarlet, they shall be as white as snow; though they be red like crimson, they shall be as wool.

Isaiah 55:7
Let the wicked forsake his way, and the unrighteous man his thoughts: and let him return unto the LORD, and he will have mercy upon him; and to our God, for he will abundantly pardon.

I John 1:9
If we confess our sins, he is faithful and just to forgive us our sins, and to cleanse us from all unrighteousness.

FORGIVING OTHERS

Matthew 6:12
And forgive us our debts, as we forgive our debtors.

Matthew 6:14
For if ye forgive men their trespasses, your heavenly Father will also forgive you.

Ephesians 4:32
And be ye kind one to another, tenderhearted, forgiving one another, even as God for Christ's sake hath forgiven you.

Colossians 3:13
Forbearing one another, and forgiving one another, if any man have a quarrel against any: even as Christ forgave you, so also do ye.

FORNICATION (Sexual intercourse outside of marriage)

I Corinthians 6:13
Meats for the belly, and the belly for meats: but God shall destroy both it and them. Now the body is not for fornication, but for the Lord; and the Lord for the body.

Galatians 5:19
Now the works of the flesh are manifest, which are these; Adultery, fornication, uncleanness, lasciviousness.

Ephesians 5:3
But fornication, and all uncleanness, or covetousness, let it not be once named among you, as becometh saints.

I Thessalonians 4:3
For this is the will of God, even your sanctification, that ye should abstain from fornication.

I Corinthians 5:9
I wrote unto you in an epistle not to company with fornicators.

FRIENDS AND FRIENDLINESS

Proverbs 18:24
A man that hath friends must shew himself friendly: and there is a friend that sticketh closer than a brother.

John 13:35
By this shall all men know that ye are my disciples, if ye have love one to another.

Galatians 6:1
Brethren, if a man be overtaken in a fault, ye which are spiritual, restore such an one in the spirit of meekness; considering thyself, lest thou also be tempted.

Galatians 6:10
As we have therefore opportunity, let us do good unto all men, especially unto them who are of the household of faith.

GROWING SPIRITUALLY

Colossians 3:16
Let the word of Christ dwell in you richly in all wisdom; teaching and admonishing one another in psalms and hymns and spiritual songs, singing with grace in your hearts to the Lord.

II Timothy 2:15
Study to shew thyself approved unto God, a workman that needeth not to be ashamed, rightly dividing the word of truth.

I Peter 2:2
As newborn babes, desire the sin-

cere milk of the word, that ye may grow thereby.

GUIDANCE

Psalm 32:8

I will instruct thee and teach thee in the way which thou shalt go: I will guide thee with mine eye.

Isaiah 30:21

And thine ears shall hear a word behind thee, saying, This is the way, walk ye in it, when ye turn to the right hand, and when ye turn to the left.

Luke 1:79

To give light to them that sit in darkness and in the shadow of death, to guide our feet in the way of peace.

HELP AND CARE

Psalm 34:7

The angel of the LORD encampeth round about them that fear him, and delivereth them.

Psalm 37:5

Commit thy way unto the LORD; trust also in him; and he shall bring it to pass.

Psalm 55:22

Cast thy burden upon the LORD, and he shall sustain thee; he shall never suffer the righteous to be moved.

Hebrews 4:16

Let us therefore come boldly unto the throne of grace, that we may obtain mercy, and find grace to help in time of need.

I Peter 5:7

Casting all your care upon him; for he careth for you.

LONELINESS

Psalm 23

Isaiah 41:10

Fear thou not; for I am with thee: be not dismayed; for I am thy God: I will strengthen thee; yea, I will help thee; yea, I will uphold thee with the right hand of my righteousness.

Hebrews 13:5

Let your conversation be without covetousness; and be content with such things as ye have: for he hath said, I will never leave thee, nor forsake thee.

LOVE (God's)

John 3:16

For God so loved the world, that he gave his only begotten Son, that whosoever believeth in him should not perish, but have everlasting life.

Romans 5:8

But God commendeth his love toward us, in that, while we were yet sinners, Christ died for us.

Romans 8:38, 39

For I am persuaded, that neither death, nor life, nor angels, nor principalities, nor powers, nor things present, nor things to come, Nor height, nor depth, nor any other creature, shall be able to separate us from the love of God, which is in Christ Jesus our Lord.

I John 3:1

Behold, what manner of love the Father hath bestowed upon us, that we should be called the sons of God: therefore the world knoweth us not, because it knew him not.

OBEDIENCE

I Samuel 15:22

And Samuel said, Hath the LORD as great delight in burnt offerings and sacrifices, as in obeying the voice of the LORD? Behold, to obey is better than sacrifice, and to hearken than the fat of rams.

Psalm 119:2

Blessed are they that keep his testimonies, and that seek him with the whole heart.

Matthew 6:24

No man can serve two masters: for either he will hate the one, and love the other; or else he will hold to the one, and despise the other. Ye cannot serve God and mammon.

John 14:21
He that hath my commandments, and keepeth them, he it is that loveth me: and he that loveth me shall be loved of my Father, and I will love him, and will manifest myself to him.

PEACE OF MIND

Isaiah 26:3
Thou wilt keep him in perfect peace, whose mind is stayed on thee: because he trusteth in thee.

John 14:27
Peace I leave with you, my peace I give unto you: not as the world giveth, give I unto you. Let not your heart be troubled, neither let it be afraid.

Romans 5:1
Therefore being justfied by faith, we have peace with God through our Lord Jesus Christ.

Colossians 3:15
And let the peace of God rule in your hearts, to the which also ye are called in one body; and be ye thankful.

PERSECUTION

Matthew 5:10
Blessed are they which are persecuted for righteousness' sake: for theirs is the kingdom of heaven.

II Timothy 3:12
Yea, and all that will live godly in Christ Jesus shall suffer persecution.

Hebrews 11:25
Choosing rather to suffer affliction with the people of God, than to enjoy the pleasures of sin for a season.

PRAISE AND GRATITUDE

I Samuel 12:24
Only fear the LORD, and serve him in truth with all your heart: for consider how great things he hath done for you.

Psalm 34:1
I will bless the LORD at all times:

his praise shall continually be in my mouth.

Psalm 139:14
I will praise thee; for I am fearfully and wonderfully made: marvelous are thy works; and that my soul knoweth right well.

PROVISION

Psalm 37:3, 4
Trust in the LORD, and do good; so shalt thou dwell in the land, and verily thou shalt be fed. Delight thyself also in the LORD; and he shall give thee the desires of thine heart.

Psalm 84:11
For the Lord God is a sun and shield: the LORD will give grace and glory: no good thing will he withhold from them that walk uprightly.

Matthew 6:33
But seek ye first the kingdom of God, and his righteousness; and all these things shall be added unto you.

Philippians 4:19
But my God shall supply all your need according to his riches in glory by Christ Jesus.

PURITY

Matthew 5:8
Blessed are the pure in heart: for they shall see God.

Psalm 24:3, 4
Who shall ascend into the hill of the LORD? or who shall stand in his holy place? He that hath clean hands, and a pure heart; who hath not lifted up his soul unto vanity, nor sworn deceitfully.

I Timothy 5:22
Lay hands suddenly on no man, neither be partaker of other men's sins: keep thyself pure.

Colossians 3:5, 6
Mortify therefore your members which are upon the earth; fornication, uncleanness, inordinate affec-

tion, evil concupiscence, and covetousness, which is idolatry.

RETURN OF CHRIST

Acts 1:11
Which also said, Ye men of Galilee, why stand ye gazing up into heaven? this same Jesus, which is taken up from you into heaven, shall so come in like manner as ye have seen him go into heaven.

I Thessalonians 4:16, 17
For the Lord himself shall descend from heaven with a shout, with the voice of the archangel, and with the trump of God: and the dead in Christ shall rise first: Then we which are alive and remain shall be caught up together with them in the clouds, to meet the Lord in the air: and so shall we ever be with the Lord.

I John 3:2
Beloved, now are we the sons of God, and it doth not yet appear what we shall be: but we know that, when he shall appear, we shall be like him; for we shall see him as he is.

SICKNESS

Psalm 119:71
It is good for me that I have been afflicted; that I might learn thy statutes.

James 5:15, 16
And the prayer of faith shall save the sick, and the Lord shall raise him up; and if he have committed sins, they shall be forgiven him. Confess your faults one to another, and pray one for another, that ye may be healed. The effectual fervent prayer of a righteous man availeth much.

SIN

Romans 3:23
For all have sinned, and come short of the glory of God.

Romans 6:23
For the wages of sin is death; but

the gift of God is eternal life through Jesus Christ our Lord.

Galatians 6:7, 8
Be not deceived; God is not mocked: for whatsoever a man soweth, that shall he also reap. For he that soweth to his flesh shall of the flesh reap corruption; but he that soweth to the Spirit shall of the Spirit reap life everlasting.

SORROW

II Corinthians 6:10
As sorrowful, yet always rejoicing; as poor, yet making many rich; as having nothing, and yet possessing all things.

Revelation 21:4
And God shall wipe away all tears from their eyes; and there shall be no more death, neither sorrow, nor crying, neither shall there be any more pain: for the former things are passed away.

STRENGTH

Deuteronomy 33:25
As thy days, so shall thy strength be.

Psalm 27:14
Wait on the LORD: be of good courage, and he shall strengthen thine heart: wait, I say, on the LORD.

Psalm 28:7
The LORD is my strength and my shield: my heart trusted in him, and I am helped: therefore my heart greatly rejoiceth; and with my song will I praise him.

Isaiah 40:29, 31
He giveth power to the faint; and to them that have no might he increaseth strength. But they that wait upon the LORD shall renew their strength; they shall mount up with wings as eagles; they shall run, and not be weary; and they shall walk, and not faint.

II Corinthians 12:9
And he said unto me, My grace is sufficient for thee: for my strength

is made perfect in weakness. Most gladly therefore will I rather glory in my infirmities, that the power of Christ may rest upon me.

SUFFERING

Romans 8:18
For I reckon that the sufferings of this present time are not worthy to be compared with the glory which shall be revealed in us.

Philippians 1:29
For unto you it is given in the behalf of Christ, not only to believe on him, but also to suffer for his sake.

II Timothy 2:12
If we suffer, we shall also reign with him: if we deny him, he also will deny us:

I Peter 4:12, 13
Beloved, think it not strange concerning the fiery trial which is to try you, as though some strange thing happened unto you: But rejoice, inasmuch as ye are partakers of Christ's sufferings; that, when his glory shall be revealed, ye may be glad also with exceeding joy.

TEMPTATION

I Corinthians 10:12, 13
Wherefore let him that thinketh he standeth take heed lest he fall. There hath no temptation taken you but such as is common to man: but God is faithful, who will not suffer you to be tempted above that ye are able; but will with the temptation also make a way to escape, that ye may be able to bear it.

Hebrews 2:18
For in that he himself hath suffered being tempted, he is able to succour them that are tempted.

James 1:14
But every man is tempted, when he is drawn away of his own lust, and enticed.

THOUGHTS

Psalm 119:11
Thy word have I hid in mine heart, that I might not sin against thee.

Proverbs 15:26
The thoughts of the wicked are an abomination to the LORD: but the words of the pure are pleasant words.

Proverbs 23:7(a)
For as he thinketh in his heart, so is he.

TRUSTING

Psalm 37:5
Commit thy way unto the LORD; trust also in him; and he shall bring it to pass.

Proverbs 3:5, 6
Trust in the LORD with all thine heart; and lean not unto thine own understanding. In all thy ways acknowledge him, and he shall direct thy paths.

VICTORY

Romans 8:37
Nay, in all these things we are more than conquerors through him that loved us.

I Corinthians 15:57
But thanks be to God, which giveth us the victory through our Lord Jesus Christ.

II Thessalonians 3:3
But the Lord is faithful, who shall stablish you, and keep you from evil.

II Timothy 2:19
Nevertheless the foundation of God standeth sure, having this seal, The Lord knoweth them that are his. And, Let every one that nameth the name of Christ depart from iniquity.

A

ACTING-OUT: Expression of unconscious emotional conflicts through overt behavior rather than internalizing these conflicts.

ADDICTION: Habitual emotional and physiological dependence upon alcohol or drugs.

ADJUSTMENT: The individual's attempts to harmonize his needs with the demands of his environment.

ADOLESCENCE: The period when a child is becoming an adult. It begins at puberty (approximately 10-14) and ends when the person comes of age (approximately 17-19).

AGGRESSION: Attack upon an object, individual or idea that stands in a person's way.

ALCOHOLISM: A diseased condition caused by the habitual use of alcohol.

AMBIVALENCE: The existence of opposing desires or feelings toward an object.

AMNESIA: Partial or total inability to recall past experiences.

ANTIDEPRESSANT DRUGS: Drugs which are used to relieve anxiety and depression.

ANTISOCIAL PERSONALITY: A person who chronically exhibits antisocial behavior.

ANXIETY: A state of being uneasy, apprehensive or worried.

APATHY: A condition marked by the absence of feeling and emotion.

APTITUDE: An inborn, potential ability to learn a specific kind of activity.

ATHETOSIS: Uncontrollable, jerky, twisting movements of the extremities.

ATROPHY: Reduction in size or wasting away of a bodily organ.

ATTITUDE: A mental set to respond in a certain manner to an object or experience.

AUTISTIC THINKING: An attempt to gratify unfulfilled desires in fantasy rather than in reality.

B

BEDWETTING (ENURESIS): Involuntary urination while asleep, continued past the usual age (4-5).

BESTIALITY: Sexual intercourse with animals.

BLOCKING: The inability to recall an idea or experience to consciousness due to emotional conflict.

C

CATHARSIS: The discharge of emotional tension associated with painful and upsetting ideas by "talking it out" with an understanding listener.

CEREBRAL PALSY: A motor disability caused by a brain dysfunction.

CHARACTER DISORDERS: Personality disorders characterized by developmental defects and lack of anxiety.

CLAUSTROPHOBIA: Morbid fear of being in small, enclosed spaces.

CLIENT-CENTERED PSYCHOTHERAPY: An approach to counseling developed chiefly by Carl Rogers. It emphasizes the importance of the client seeking his own solutions rather than being actively directed by the counselor.

COMPENSATION: A defense mechanism by which an individual covers up an undesirable trait by exaggerating a desirable one.

COMPULSION: An irresistible urge to perform some act even though the individual realizes it is irrational.

CONCUSSION: An injury to the head or spine which causes rupturing of small blood vessels in the brain. This may cause circulatory disturbances, tissue damage, shock and unconsciousness.

CONFLICT: Stress characterized by incompatible desires, needs or environmental demands.

D

DAYDREAMING: Wishful or purposeless thinking during waking hours. A form of fantasy.

DEFENSE MECHANISMS: Ways of dealing with ego-involving conflicts. They are attempts to protect and enhance the person's self-concept.

DELINQUENCY: Illegal or antisocial behavior engaged in by a minor.

DELUSION: A belief which is out of keeping with reality and the individual's level of maturity.

DENIAL: A defense mechanism by which a person avoids unpleasant emotional conflicts by denying or refusing to perceive some aspect of reality.

DEPRESSION: Undue sadness, dejection or melancholy. Feelings of worthlessness and guilt and, often, of apprehension.

DIAGNOSIS: Identification of the nature and extent of a disorder by an analysis of the symptoms.

DRUG ADDICTION: Habitual emotional and physiological dependence upon drugs.

DRUG THERAPY: The use of drugs in treating mental illness.

DUAL PERSONALITY: A dissociative reaction in which a person exhibits different personality structures.

DYNAMICS: The determination of the causes and effects of an emotional or behavioral pattern.

DYSFUNCTION: Impaired functioning of an organ.

DYSSOCIAL REACTION: Antisocial behavior resulting from living in an abnormal moral environment.

E

EGO: The conscious part of personality which mediates between the individual's impulses and the demands of reality; the self.

EGOCENTRIC: Preoccupied with one's own concerns; self-centered.

ELECTROENCEPHALOGRAPH (EEG): An apparatus for recording the electrical activity of the brain.

ELECTROSHOCK THERAPY: The administration of a carefully regulated electrical current to the brain in the treatment of severe mental disorders.

EMOTIONAL IMMATURITY: Inadequate development of adult emotional control in areas such as independence and self-reliance. The use of childish behavior to meet stresses which most people can handle satisfactorily.

EMOTIONAL INSULATION: A defense mechanism in which the individual reduces anxiety by withdrawal and refusal to become emotionally involved with others.

EMPATHY: An insightful awareness and understanding of the feelings, emotions and behavior of another person.

ENCEPHALITIS: Inflammation of the brain.

ENDOCRINE GLANDS: The glands of internal secretion. They secrete hormones which regulate body functions and growth.

ENDOCRINOLOGIST: A medical doctor who specializes in the treatment of the endocrine glands and the internal secretions of the body.

ENURESIS: Involuntary urination while asleep, continued past the usual age (4-5).

ENVIRONMENT: The world a person lives in, such as home, school, office, family, church and other social contacts.

EPILEPSY: A chronic disease of the nervous system, characterized by convulsions and often unconsciousness.

EROTIC: Pertaining to sexual stimulation.

ETIOLOGY: The investigation of the causes of a disorder.

EUNUCH: A male who has been castrated or whose testes have never developed.

EXHIBITIONISM: Public exposure of the sex organs.

EXTROVERT: A person whose interests are directed toward his environment rather than toward inner experiences and himself.

F

FABRICATION: Telling of imaginary events or stories as if they were true; confabulation.

FAMILIAL: Relating to characteristics which run in families.

FANTASY: A defense mechanism by which an individual escapes from the world of reality and seeks gratification through imaginary activities; daydreaming.

FEEBLEMINDEDNESS: Mental deficiency; mental capacity considerably below average.

FORNICATION: Sexual relations outside of marriage.

FREE-FLOATING ANXIETY: Anxiety which is not attached to any specific object. It occurs in all situations.

FRUSTRATION: Thwarting of a person's efforts to satisfy basic needs and drives.

FUNCTIONAL: An illness which has no organic or structural basis; psychogenic.

G

GENERAL PARESIS: Mental illness associated with degeneration of the brain due to syphilitic infection.

GENETICS: The branch of science dealing with heredity.

GERIATRICS: The science which studies and treats the aged.

GIGANTISM: A condition of abnormal size due to oversecretion of the pituitary gland.

GROUP THERAPY: Counseling or psychotherapy with a group of patients.

GUILT: Feelings of apprehension and sinfulness. A distinction must be made between real guilt which is induced by the Holy Spirit for transgression of God's law, and pseudo guilt which arises from an overly-critical environment.

H

HALLUCINATION: Sense perception which does not have an external stimulus.

HEREDITY: Genetic transmission of characteristics from parents to their offspring.

HETEROSEXUALITY: Attraction, interest and physical relationships between individuals of the opposite sex.

HOMOSEXUALITY: Inverted sexual orientation. Sexual attraction or relationships between members of the same sex.

HOSTILITY: An emotion or feeling of enmity, ill-will, unfriendliness or antagonism.

HYPNOSIS: An artificially induced state resembling sleep, in which the person is more fully influenced by suggestion.

I

ID: A term used to denote a person's unconscious, instinctual urges.

IDIOT: A severely mentally-retarded person. Usually denotes an I.Q. score below 25.

IMBECILE: A mentally-retarded individual with an I.Q. score between 25 and 49.

IMPULSE: An urge to action which has little forethought or anticipation.

INCEST: Sexual intercourse between two closely related individuals such as brother and sister or father and daughter.

INCOMPETENT: A lack of the mental qualifications needed to manage one's own affairs. This may be due to either mental illness or mental deficiency.

INFANTILISM: The presence of immature and childish behavior in an adult.

INFERIORITY COMPLEX: A person's feeling that he is inadequate and doesn't measure up to desired standards.

INSIGHT: The sudden recognition of the cause or solution to a problem. The discernment of relationships between data or experiences.

INTELLECTUALIZATION: A defense mechanism in which the individual avoids emotional hurt by substituting an intellectual for an emotional interpretation of a threatening situation.

INTROPUNITIVE: Responding to frustration by blaming oneself.

INTROVERT: A person is quiet and reflective rather than interested in his external environment.

J

JUVENILE DELINQUENCY: Antisocial and illegal behavior by minors.

K

KLEPTOMANIA: An irresistable compulsion to steal. The individual frequently has no need for the stolen object.

M

MALADJUSTMENT: The inability to adapt to problems and tasks of everyday life.

MANIC-DEPRESSIVE REACTION: A psychotic disorder characterized by extreme mood disturbances. Manic states evidence excitability and overactivity while depressive states are characterized by dejection and underactivity.

MASTURBATION: Sexual gratification through self-stimulation of the genitals.

MENTAL AGE (MA): A measure of an individual's intellectual development. A mental age of eight, for example, means that the person has the intellectual ability of an average eight-year-old child.

MONGOLISM: A form of mental deficiency which is characterized by facial features resembling the Mongolian race.

N

NERVOUS BREAKDOWN: A popular term referring to a variety of emotional disturbances which interfere with a person's ability to deal adequately with daily activities.

NERVOUSNESS: A condition characterized by tension, apprehension and restlessness.

NEUROLOGIST: Medical doctor who specializes in the diagnosis and treatment of diseases of the brain and nervous system.

NONDIRECTIVE THERAPY: An approach to counseling developed by Carl Rogers. It emphasizes the importance of the client seeking his own solutions rather than being actively directed by the therapist.

O

OBSESSION: Persistent, irresistible idea or thought which an individual cannot remove from consciousness.

OBSESSIVE-COMPULSIVE REACTION: Psychoneurotic reaction characterized by persistent thoughts and uncontrollable impulses to perform a certain act.

OPIUM: A drug which leads to physiological and psychological dependence. It is prepared from a type of poppy. Major derivatives of opium are morphine, heroin, paregoric and codeine.

OUT-PATIENT CLINIC: Clinic where individuals are treated on a non-hospitalized basis.

OVERPROTECTION: Sheltering a child from all possible dangers to such a degree that he is unable to stand on his own.

P

PARANOIA: A psychotic mental disorder characterized by well-systematized delusions of persecution or grandeur.

PASSIVE-AGGRESSIVE REACTION: Aggressiveness which is expressed in a quiet manner such as pouting, stubbornness or inefficiency.

PERFECTIONISM: Excessive attention to detail. This behavior often serves as a defense against feelings of insecurity and guilt.

PERSONALITY: The sum total of a person's attitudes, drives, aspirations, strengths, weaknesses, interests and abilities.

PERVERSION: Deviation from normal. Often used in a limited fashion to denote sexual abnormality.

PLAY THERAPY: Use of play activities in therapy with children. It enables a child to act out his feelings in an accepting environment.

PRENATAL: Before birth.

PROGNOSIS: A judgment concerning the duration, course and outcome of a pathological condition.

PROJECTION: Defense mechanism in which an individual places blame for his difficulties upon others or ascribes his own unacceptable impulses to others.

PSYCHIATRIC SOCIAL WORK: Social work primarily concerned with the mentally ill.

PSYCHIATRIST: Medical doctor who deals with mental and emotional disorders.

PSYCHOANALYSIS: The method of approach to human behavior originally outlined by Sigmund Freud. This approach places emphasis on unconscious processes. It comprises a theory of personality development and functioning and repressed experiences in the formations of psychotherapeutic techniques, and research techniques for the mental disorders.

PSYCHOLOGICAL TEST: Standardized examinations designed to yield information on an individual's mental and emotional adjustment.

PSYCHOLOGY: The branch of science which deals with human behavior and adjustment.

PSYCHOSIS: Severe form of mental illness characterized by loss of contact with reality. Delusions and hallucinations may also be present.

PSYCHOTHERAPY: The use of psychological techniques in treating emotional disturbances.

PUBERTY: The beginning of adolescence. The time when the reproductive functions mature.

R

RAPPORT: Empathic relationship between two individuals characterized by mutual cooperation and confidence. Used in psychology to denote a desirable patient-therapist relationship.

REFERRAL: Sending a person to another specialist for diagnosis or treatment.

REALITY: The world as it actually is. The ability to correctly perceive reality is impaired in some forms of mental illness.

REPRESSION: Defense mechanism by which a person forces threatening ideas or impulses into the unconscious mind.

ROLE PLAYING: Technique of psychotherapy in which the individual acts out a conflict situation in order to gain insight into his behavior.

S

SCHIZOPHRENIA: Psychotic disorder characterized by loss of contact with reality, confused thought processes and withdrawal.

SECURITY: A sense of safety and ability to meet the needs of life.

SELF-CONCEPT: A person's attitudes toward his personal worth.

SELF-DEVALUATION: Self-criticism associated with feelings of unworthiness.

SENILITY: Mental and psychological deterioration with old age.

SEXUAL DEVIATION: Any perversion of sexual behavior.

SHOCK THERAPY: Use of convulsive drugs such as insulin or metrazol, or electro-shock in treating mental disorders.

SOMATIC: Pertaining to the body.

SPASTIC: A person who lacks normal coordination because of dysfunctions of the brain.

STRESS: A condition which is threatening to an individual's adjustment.

STRESS TOLERANCE: The amount of stress which a person can handle without developing serious personality disturbances.

STUTTERING: Speech disorder characterized by a disturbance in the rhythm of speech. This may include either blocking (inability to articulate certain sounds) or repetition of a sound.

SUBCONSCIOUS: Mental activities which are outside an individual's awareness or consciousness.

SUBLIMATION: Defense mechanism in which an unacceptable drive is channeled into socially acceptable activities.

T

TENSION: A condition characterized by anxiety, suspense or strain.

THERAPEUTIC: Related to treatment or healing of maladjustments.

THERAPY: Procedure designed to treat maladjustments.

TIC: Persistent, intermittent muscle twitch or spasm.

TRANSFERENCE: Unconscious attachment of attitude to a person who represents a significant figure in the person's past.

U

UNCONSCIOUS: That portion of the mind of which a person is unaware.

UNCONSCIOUS MOTIVATION: Incentive or drive of which a person is unaware.

W

WITHDRAWAL: A tendency to retreat from one's environment, usually because of feelings of insecurity.

WITHDRAWAL SYMPTOMS: Physical and emotional symptoms resulting from the removal of a drug from an addicted individual.